FIVE GOLD RINGS

To John and Una

with our love and thanks

May and Marcus

Christmas 2003.

FIVE GOLD RINGS

Powerful influences on prominent people

Edited by
ANNA JEFFERY

DARTON · LONGMAN + TODD

First published in 2003 by
Darton, Longman and Todd Ltd
1 Spencer Court
140–142 Wandsworth High Street
London SW18 4JJ

Individual contributions © 2003 individual contributors
Collection © 2003 Anna Jeffery

ISBN 0–232–52528–5

A catalogue record for this book is available from the British Library.

Set in 10.75/13pt Bembo
Designed and produced by Sandie Boccacci
using QuarkXPress on an Apple PowerMac

Printed and bound in Great Britain by
The Cromwell Press, Trowbridge, Wiltshire

Robert
With deep gratitude

CONTENTS

FOREWORD

What makes people? Helps to shape and form their lives? Influences career moves? How important are those early parental influences?

Could it be a particular person we have met? A book we have read? A place of special significance or special charm? Some haunting lines of poetry? How open and receptive are we to God's guiding hand through such profound influences?

I have come to believe there is a golden thread of guidance running through our lives – if only we have eyes to see – which is epitomised by outstanding people we meet, books we read, a place we cannot forget, lines of poetry that haunt us – all of which can be crystallised in our philosophy of life.

With this in mind, a year or so ago I invited a number of contemporary luminaries to demonstrate this by writing about the person, book, place and poem which have most inspired them, and from these and other influences, to draw out their philosophy of life. *Five Gold Rings: powerful influences on prominent people* is the result. A captivating collection of people's frank confessions of what has helped shape their lives, helped them become the people they are, helped their beliefs to form. An absorbing, enriching collection for anyone interested in what makes people. Shining evidence of that golden thread.

It is my hope that this book may prove to be an inspiration for you to consider what might be *your* five gold rings and perhaps recognise for the first time the golden thread running through your own life.

ANNA JEFFERY
March 2003

ABOUT THE EDITOR

Anna Jeffery lives in Surrey with her architect husband Michael. She has a background of health service administration combined with a deeply held Christian faith; for many years she has been aware of an inner drive to help others come to that same shared faith. In 1992 she launched Cultural Country Retreats, a national network of retreats 'with a difference' primarily for those on the fringe of the church who were seeking a spiritual dimension to their lives. These retreats were held at some of the finest retreat houses in the UK, providing a cultural and rural framework within which spiritual thought and reflection could take place. The blend of rural setting, musical input (retreats ran alongside a number of classical music festivals) and buildings of rich historical interest, together with the spiritual dimension, enriched the lives of all who participated. The retreats, which ran for ten years, are currently being restructured.

This is Anna's first venture into publishing. A spiritual anthology, *Symphony of Life*, is her next challenge. Unusually creative, she is driven by a desire to help those preoccupied with material wealth and values to seek instead a Christian faith, which she believes is the only stabilising factor in this violent and unstable world – the only wealth worth seeking.

Future projects on the drawing board include *Oxford Visions* (a national network of discussion groups in association with the re-formatted Cultural Country Retreats), *Double Vision* (the exploration of faith in identical twins) and the establishment of a lay community.

ACKNOWLEDGEMENTS

I am indebted to all our contributors who have given so generously and unsparingly of their time – without them, of course, there would be no Gold Rings and my vision would still be on the drawing board.

I would like to thank those who have given permission to reproduce extracts from the publications in the Epilogue (see notes). Every effort has been made to trace the copyright owners of each extract. In cases where the source is unknown to the compiler, I would be glad to hear from the copyright owner and due acknowledgement will be made in all future editions of the book. If there are any inadvertent omissions in the acknowledgements, I apologise to those concerned.

In addition, my thanks are due to:

J. M. Dent for permission to reprint *The Bright Field* by R. S. Thomas from *Collected Poems*

The Carcanet Press Ltd for permission to reprint extracts from *From Bourgeois Land* by Iain Crichton Smith from *Selected Poems*

Margaret Hichens for permission to reprint 'Friends' from *Living in an HIV+ World: South African Stories of Pain and Hope*, ed. D. Genrich and P. Sherrifs

A. P. Watt Ltd, on behalf of the Executors of the Estate of Jocelyn Herbert and Teresa Elizabeth Perkins for permission to reprint 'A Certain School in Days Gone By' by A. P. Herbert from *The Book of Ballads: Collected Light Verse*, 1948

Terry Falla for permission to reprint 'He is Hidden' and 'Be Our Freedom Lord'

I am indebted to Virginia Hearn and her team at Darton, Longman and Todd who have given such warm support to a fledgling writer and to the Trustees of the Cultural Country Retreats Trust who have loyally backed this new venture and under whose auspices this book is published. My thanks are due to Denis Duncan for all his help, support and encouragement in the early stages and to dear Robert Llewelyn without whose vast experience and theological expertise this book would surely never have become a reality. And last but not least, I am indebted to my long-suffering husband Michael – his endless patience with a bear of little mechanical brain (who much prefers the quill pen to modern-day technology) made it possible for this book to reach the publishers on time so that it could be in your hands today.

ANNA JEFFERY
March 2003

SIMON BARRINGTON-WARD

Simon Barrington-Ward trained for ordination at Westcott House, Cambridge and became Chaplain of Magdalene College, Cambridge in 1956. He lectured at the University of Ibadan, Nigeria in the early 60s before returning to Magdalene, Cambridge as Fellow and Dean of Chapel until 1969. He served as Principal of Crowther Hall, a Church Missionary Society training college, in Birmingham and then became General Secretary of CMS, a post which he held for ten years. He was installed as Bishop of Coventry in 1985 and remained there until 1997. He was made a Knight of the Order of St Michael and St George in 2001 and is currently Assistant Bishop of Ely and Honorary Fellow and Honorary Assistant Chaplain of Magdalene College, Cambridge.

The Person

Viola Garvin

My parents surely shaped my mind and heart and gave me a frame-work of values underpinned by a sense of God, but Viola Garvin, 'Aunt' Viola to me, loomed gently over my childhood and youth like the long-drawn angel holding a sundial on the tower of Chartres Cathedral, a picture of which she cherished. She added to life another vivid dimension of a kind of mystery and presence. She herself was tall and slender, always wearing long flowing skirts of grey or black, and often a jacket and tricorn hat to match, with touches of a distinctive greyish-blue that still recalls her instantly. Her almost 'gamin'-like face, with striking grey-blue eyes, that gazed at you and looked through and beyond you, and her small, firm chin, stay vividly with me. I recall her way of gently murmuring 'mmm' as I prattled on, and then suddenly responding to something I'd said with interest or an amusement that was both tender and shrewd. Her conversation was, like the postcards she sent, written with a broad nib in a big, sweeping hand, her comments always unexpected: after guests had gone, 'Parties are such sweet sorrow!' or, when I had written from school after a long gap, 'Simon, you are like God, your silences are so immense; your communications so delightful!' She was vague but at the same time swift and direct, as when ringing up my home, 'Is that your Mother?'

Her husband was a phenomenal journalist, J. L. Garvin, Editor of *The Observer*, my father's former chief and my brother's godfather. To visit them, as my brother and I did often, one entered through an opening out of an ordinary suburban street, plunged into a tunnel of trees and emerged beside a long, ramshackle, ivy-clad, old farmhouse, called 'Gregories', surrounded by grass, with woods and a lake. At one end of the L-shaped house, 'Garve' reigned in the lofty shepherds' kitchen with its great window, strikingly large in his dressing gown, his prominent eyes glowing like his cigar, half mystic, half political orator. At the other end was Aunt Viola, in her long, bow-windowed drawing room, with Italianate and French touches. Upstairs her bedroom had stars on its blue ceiling, as in George Macdonald's *The Princess and Curdie*. She had a touch of her Pre-Raphaelite background and of the French Catholicism which had won her. In the middle of the house in the long dining room, at opposite ends of the refectory table Garve thundered and Viola gazed on quizzically. When I had quoted a line of poetry about there being in God 'a deep but dazzling darkness', Garve struck the board so that the green glasses rattled and shouted, 'No! (*pause*) No! God is light and in him is there no darkness at all!' 'Both are true, Garve!' Aunt Viola said.

After he had died and the great house had been broken up, she moved to where we now lived and re-created something of the old feel of her side of Gregories in North Oxford. There, in frequent conversations she regaled me with stories of people she loved and many a saying. She introduced me to Julian of Norwich and talked of love and forgiveness. She showed me what it means, to quote a poem of hers, 'to live with vision, courage and no hate!'

The Book

The Brothers Karamazov

Once, when I was visiting Volgograd (formerly Stalingrad) and was talking with the Archbishop, German, about the way in which some of the contrasts of poverty and wealth, the spiritual and ethical vacuum, and the uncertainties in the lives of so many of the people I met reminded me of Dostoevsky's Russia, he replied, 'What we need is a new Optino.' This struck me deeply since I knew that the monastery in *The Brothers Karamazov* and its elder ('staretz', spiritual guide) were partly modelled on Optino and its famous elder, Amvrosy, both of whom Dostoevsky and Tolstoy, in common with so many others of all classes, visited in search of spiritual guidance. The story presents vividly what for me has seemed since my Berlin time, the underlying and crucial drama of our time, our need and struggle for that true social and spiritual reality we can only find in God, a reality opened up to us in those people who genuinely reflect Christ.

Dostoevsky was approaching the social and spiritual crisis of his time, of which the harshness of family life and the plight of many children seemed to him a symptom, through the members of the Karamazov family. From the main opening scene in book II onwards, the amoral and depraved father of the Karamazov family and his two older sons epitomise the problem. Dmitri, unstable, uncherished, dissipated, passionate and violent, is yet underneath conscience stricken and wanting some kind of order in his life. Ivan, fanatically rationalistic, is attracted by the logic of applying the Christian ideal at its noblest, and yet unable to believe in God or immortality which he recognises leads to naked self-interest and egoism. Indeed Ivan becomes the darkly arrogant and cold individualist, embodying the whole romantic revolution against God. He mounts the most devastating assault on Christian belief, which contains his famous tale of the Grand Inquisitor. Dostoevsky confessed in a letter that 'in Europe there never had been so power-ful an expression of atheism', characteristic of the kind of atheistic socialist reformers and radicals he himself had known.

'I tremble', he wrote, 'for my attempt to give an answer', asking, 'Will it be a sufficient answer?'

That answer is presented in the person of the youngest son, Alyosha, with behind him his beloved elder, Zosima, who, even in the opening scene, penetratingly perceives the spiritual conflict deep within Ivan, and more accessibly within Dmitri, and looks shrewdly and compassionately on both. For Dostoevsky, the entirely coherent and 'Euclidean' atheism of Ivan can only be countered adequately and totally by those who, in their freely given, self-sacrificing love, empowered by the Spirit of Christ within them, forgiven all and forgiving all, are transfigured into living icons of our true meaning and destiny. They present a different world. In the spiritual move-ment generated by an Amvrosy and his disciples (a movement, it so happens, with the Jesus Prayer at its heart), a movement of deep prayer and radical compassionate action, as it is embodied in Alyosha and those among the children in the moving final scene of the book, Dostoevsky gives us a glimpse of the future which purified hearts alone can bring in. For me certainly, as for his contemporaries and many since, Dostoevsky has made this wholeness through broken-ness, this alternative to the terrible fate hanging over humanity and the creation itself, lastingly compelling.

The Place

Berlin 1953

'Berlin! Berlin! Berlin! – immer daran denken!' (always think of it). This slogan, on a label stuck to the window of the carriage in the train on which I left the city after eighteen momentous months which had changed my life, drew tears from me.

On the June day in 1953, on which I arrived from Cambridge after three years there, I would never have guessed I might feel like that. It had been cloudy as the plane dipped over the city towards Templehof. For the first time I saw those ruins stretching to the horizon, the empty windows in hollow facades opening into a void, the Brandenburg gate, an entrance from nowhere into nowhere, in a lunar landscape of bleached rubble and dust. True, I was soon welcomed and taken to the pleasant green suburb of Dahlem, where the new Free University had come into being, in which I was to give lectures in English. Not far was the Grunewald, with its woods and lakes. My kindly landlady became a friend. Over the coming months I had students in to tea and became part of the Englisch–Amerikanisches Seminar. But I struggled to speak enough German, and at times felt lonely. And as the autumn drew on into winter and the leaves blew down the streets, I went on walks through the grey mounds of rubble by the sluggish river, until that sad disintegration seemed to be closing in on me.

My fellow lodger, cut off from his family in the East, and dis-illusioned with the Nazism in which he had been schooled, had become sharply and brilliantly sceptical. He tore to pieces my rather frail and confused idealism and mocked my beliefs until he made them seem unreal.

At this point, a kindly older woman, a neighbour, took me to a reading of contemporary poets in a nearby house. On stepping in I found myself in one of those heart-warming places that restore you. It was warm and colourful, its modern furniture made by the pastor, its abstract paintings by his wife! In a basement refectory the poems sprang out and gripped us as they were read. I felt at home in this a group of people of all backgrounds and ages. There was a great openness and acceptance, and an atmosphere of what I could only call forgiven-ness. One man admitted, 'I was a Nazi' whilst others from the church had been secretly opposed to Hitler. When they invited me to return for Bible study, I was hooked.

Friendships multiplied in and through this wonderfully creative group. I went out to work in refugee hostels, to political meetings about the future of the city and a pattern of society beyond communism and capitalism. I heard a disciple of Bonhoeffer speak and was drawn into inspiring worship with these new friends. I met with Christians in East and West, and went with them to the Brecht ensemble or the opera. Among them I began to discern the person and power of Christ as 'mitmensch', God with and for us. He became the root of a flowering in the winter city, a way beyond East and West, a movement in his Spirit of breaking and re-making, life through death, growth through forgiven-ness into love, which Berlin, like Dresden later in my life, would always symbolise for me.

The Poem

That Nature is a Heraclitean Fire and of the comfort of the Resurrection – Gerard Manley Hopkins

When I was leaving school and my father died, I first read this poem and was overwhelmed by it and realised how deeply it spoke to me of the way in which the tragic transience and ebbing away of life alone can be countered. I came to love this pattern of reversal in some of George Herbert's poems such as *Affliction I, The Collar* and *The Flower* in which one tiny couplet at the end can turn the whole poem right round.

In this poem it is also a kind of transcending of nature, a resistance which shines out against the dark, that opens up the promise of a new destiny for the whole creation. Heraclitus' philosophical fragments suggest that life is a cyclical process of constant flux, as the underlying fire (a kind of 'hot wind' not unlike the 'energy' now seen to be constituting all matter). Water either evaporates to form more 'fire' or dries to become earth, while some earth and fire dissolve or condense into water. The soul similarly composed of fire can also be destroyed by sin.

So, in the poem, clouds that in their varying shapes scamper ('chevy') along air-built thoroughfares show this flux of life, the play of sharp flashes of light and tracery of shadow on walls and trees. The 'bright wind', like the Heraclitean fire itself, dries the mud into dust, stops the flow of water and stiffens the ooze into a 'footfretted' crust of earth. This amazing, solitary poet, with his wonderful, magical power to shape a language more closely embodying the processes of life than that of any of his contemporaries, prepared his spells, still unaware how many would be transfixed by them in time to come. With poignant compassion he helps us sense this flow into dissolution of all life, in 'nature's bonfire, drowning all, supremely her bonniest, dearest to her, her clearest-selved spark', the human being. The one being that seemed to stand out, distinct and separate as a star, 'death blots black out', with all else swept away.

At this moment there shines out like a trumpet sound, a new sign, the risen one, shining uncomprehended through the dark, 'The Resurrection, a heart's-clarion!' Grief and dejection vanish.

> Across my foundering deck shone
> A beacon, an eternal beam.

Even though 'flesh fade' and 'mortal trash fall to the residuary worm', Hopkins' transcending conclusion of our being united with Christ in his rising, is surely one of the great moments in all poetry:

> I am all at once what Christ is, since he was what I am, and
> This Jack, joke, poor potsherd, patch, matchwood, immortal
>   diamond,
> Is immortal diamond.

This exchange, whereby God in Christ entered into our life and death, our flux and our falling to dust, that we might, through trust in him, enter again and again into his death and risen life, leads us into the rhythm of being constantly broken and remade as we keep reaching out for the final wholeness, God's kingdom. Like Alyosha and his teacher Zosima we can all of us reflect the light of the risen one and thus open up to our world a new hope. This poem came to epitomise the constant movement of the Spirit through apparent failing and falling only to keep rising again into the new creation, already beginning, here and now.

My Philosophy of Life

There is an Orthodox saying that 'the true theologian is one who prays'.

I would believe this includes also 'the true philosopher'. That is to say that out of our prayer our philosophy emerges. Once I stepped into a monastery chapel where the Jesus Prayer was being led by one voice, saying 'Lord Jesus Christ, have mercy on us' (the corporate version) as visitors, nuns and monks, gathered round, were silently drawn into the prayer together. I sensed that we were touching on a rhythm running through all life, a cosmic rhythm of continuous homecoming and journeying, constantly arriving at our goal and constantly reaching out to let it grasp us more. As Paul put it, 'I reach out to grasp that which in Christ has already grasped me.' (Philippians 3:12)

So this means that we must start our journey, like our prayer, at the end. This is what revealed itself in the Garvins' house or in a bluebell wood in childhood when I put my hand on a tree. As I gazed, everything became one and the people, moving through the woods and the waves of flowers stretching beyond them, all became part of that unity. Time was suspended, until a voice summoned me and I rose reluctantly, broke through the surface and was back in the ordinary world. But much later I realised that when we come into the presence of the risen Christ and surrender ourselves to him, that oneness, lost sight of since childhood, begins to be restored as we are brought into his love. This is the moment of 'Lord Jesus Christ, Son of God . . . '

But then we have to face the fractured state of our hearts, our families and communities, our society, our world. We can only move from that shattered condition towards our true human destiny, a rightly ordered society, holding together freedom for all with justice for each, especially the weakest and the poorest, growing in love and truth, through a journey of continuous repentance and forgiveness. This means a mutual honesty and humbling and confessing our own wrong, a release of profound acceptance and forgiveness. We need this in our marriages, in our family life, between parents and children, in the places where we work or live. We need it in our society, a politics of forgiveness, where no one party or person is completely right or wrong and all work together to utilise the ideas, skills and gifts of each. We need it desperately internationally and between North and South, East and West. We need it in and between our faith communities, since people of all faiths can converge upon this continuing redemptive process. This is the moment of 'have mercy upon us'.

Ultimately we need to discover together and each in our own heart that fusion of homecoming and journeying, contemplation and intercession, joyful mourning, being at peace, and yet longing and working for peace for all, being 'still and still moving', which is the secret of great literature, great art, and great music, which, as Karl Barth said of Mozart, 'sees the light of eternity no more than we do, but hears the whole world enveloped in that light'. So the love which holds us is also the love which draws us ever deeper and further into the redemptive process in this world and in the world to come.

MARCUS BRAYBROOKE

Presently vicar of the Baldons with Nuneham Courtenay near Oxford, Marcus Braybrooke has been involved in interfaith work for over thirty-five years and has travelled widely. A former Director of the Council of Christians and Jews, he was one of the founders of the Three Faiths Forum and of the International Interfaith Centre of which he is now a Patron. He is also President of the World Congress of Faiths. He has written several books on Christianity, Christian–Jewish relations and interfaith subjects.

The Person

George Appleton

George Appleton is the person, apart from Mary my wife and my parents, who has influenced me most. He stimulated my interest in other faiths, suggested I should succeed him as chair of the World Congress of Faiths, confirmed our two children and when for health reasons I had to take early retirement, he found some money so that I could buy an Amstrad word-processor and a photocopier which got me started as an author and now, like him, I am editing anthologies of prayers. A great traveller, George never tired in his exploration of faith and the mystery of the Divine.

It was as a student that I first heard him speak at the USPG annual meeting for missionary candidates, which was held each year in January at High Leigh. My main memory is of the freezing chapel – what a lot of time I have spent in chilly churches! – but a more significant memory is of a conference at which he, Kenneth Cragg and Dr Basu spoke of the exciting prospect of intellectual encounter and convergence between the religions of the world – and that has been my life's greatest interest.

Soon after ordination, I joined the World Congress of Faiths and quickly became Honorary Secretary. On the death of Lord Sorensen George Appleton became Chairman, although he was still Archbishop in Jerusalem – in the interim the President Edward Carpenter took the chair. George suggested that WCF – which meant me – should arrange an interfaith pilgrimage and conference

in Jerusalem, which was a fascinating introduction to Christian–
Jewish dialogue, the first of the pilgrimages/tours that I have led and
probably the first ever interfaith tour. The return flight was much
delayed because of Israeli airforce manoeuvres so I had a good
chance to get to know Marjorie Appleton.

When George returned to Britain, he played an active part in
WCF. With Swami Bhavyanada of the Ramakrishna Movement we
arranged the first interfaith meditation retreats and tried to persuade
religions to work and pray together for peace. At WCF's fortieth
anniversary service at Canterbury Cathedral, George declared that
each religion had good news for all people.

He visited our various homes. When he preached at our church
at Frindsbury in Kent, I first discovered that archbishops are very
human and like their whisky. George also wanted a kettle in his
room as he got up very early to spend long hours in prayer. He
confirmed our two children in a lovely service at Swainswick.

My prayer life has been deeply influenced by his books and
example. They have an honesty which is always refreshing and touch
on many vital concerns. He helped me learn the importance of
silence and contemplation. As he became more physically infirm, he
often telephoned to ask how we were and when possible we visited
him at Oxford. His mind was as active as ever and he talked about
the new books which I should read and which he had already
annotated in his neat writing.

We are not asked which prayer has most inspired us, but these
words of George sum up his commitment and his influence:

> O God of many names,
> Lover of all people,
> Give peace
> in our hearts,
> in our homes,
> in our world,
> in our universe.
> The peace of our need,
> The peace of your will.

The Book

The Bible

Since I was about 15 I have read at least one chapter of the Bible almost every day. If I choose the Bible as the book that has had the most profound influence on my life, I realise that as a clergyman I am open to the comment, 'he would say that, wouldn't he?' Maybe, as on a desert island, I should assume the Bible and Shakespeare are taken for granted.

The Bible has introduced me to an amazing sweep of human history – from the ancient Pharaohs to Cyrus, from Alexander the Great to the Emperor Augustus. It has encouraged me to lead tours not only to the Holy Land but also in the steps of St Paul to Greece and Turkey and thus encouraged me to learn about many ancient civilisations. It even made me struggle to learn Greek.

The Bible, especially in the Psalms, grapples with the whole range of human emotions. Like *The News of the World*, all life is in the Bible and God is achieving the divine purpose in the muddle of human struggles. Above all, of course, the Bible introduces us to the figure of Jesus, in whom I see most clearly revealed the compassion and forgiveness of God. Attempts to form a clearer picture of the historical Jesus have fascinated me and have been relevant to attempts to build a better relationship between Jews and Christians. I see Jesus as a faithful Jew, even if like the prophets he put righteousness above ritual. The parting of the ways between church and synagogue happened some time after his death and although God may have used it, I doubt whether it was Jesus' intention. Today the shared study of scripture has become an effective way of bringing Jews and Christians – and Muslims as well – together. My appreciation of the Hebrew scriptures has been enriched by reading Jewish commentaries.

It is fascinating to compare the various translations of the scriptures, although I still tend to remember passages as they are in the Authorised Version, which is useful as I have inherited from a clerical ancestor an early edition of *Cruden's Concordance*. It is usually also to the Authorised Version that poets and hymn writers allude.

Most Sundays I have preached at least one sermon and scripture always has something new to say. It is like a well with an unending spring of water. But vital as it is, the Bible as Word of God points beyond itself to the Living Word who is Christ and needs to be interpreted in his light. The Bible invites us to a conversation with the Living Lord.

> How sweet are thy words unto my taste!
> Yea, sweeter than honey to my mouth.
>
> (Psalm 119:104)

The Place

Madras Christian College

Our bank, as a security check, asks for a memorable address and I give the house where I grew up. Galilee and the Holy Land come high on the list of unforgettable places, as for other reasons do Auschwitz and Hiroshima, but India has had the most lasting influence and particularly Madras Christian College at Tambaram.

I spent nearly a year there as soon as I had finished at Cambridge – not even waiting for the degree ceremony. Chandran Devanesen, the first Indian principal, welcomed me warmly and almost immediately Mrs Devanesen took me to buy a bed, although everyone else in the student hostel slept on the floor. That was the only concession for a westerner. I soon learned to appreciate Indian vegetarian food and to enjoy all the religious festivals when we had special meals.

It was a joy to be a guest member of the Church of South India and I would like to have been ordained there, but that was too much for the authorities of the Church of England, but I have never been at ease with denominationalism. I spent Christmas in a remote village in Andhra Pradesh and saw how Christianity had brought new life and hope to those who had been outcasts. My professor, Dr C. T. K. Chari, invited me to his home for many Hindu festivals and for endless conversation. He introduced me to Hindu thought, especially Sri Ramakrishna who claimed on the basis of his spiritual experience that all religions lead to God, to Idealist philosophers and to mysticism, both East and West. He also arranged for me to stay with several Brahmin families in South India. This helped me to appreciate how people lived their Hinduism in a fast-changing society. I also stayed in Delhi with his brother, a convert to Christianity, who was a senior member of the railway board. He in turn arranged for his colleagues to provide me with hospitality at Lucknow and Varanasi and Agra – I became very experienced at travelling third class across India and always tried to get the top bunk, so as to escape from questions about my name and how much I earned (which was nil!). I was also received by Dr Radhakrishnan, the President of India, who had studied at Madras Christian College and who later was to become Patron of the World Congress of Faiths. My travels also took me to Murray and Mary Roger's ashram in Jyotiniketan, where I learned that the exterior dialogue with members of another faith has to be accompanied by an interior dialogue with the Lord.

No one can escape India's poverty. It has made me a lifelong supporter of Christian Aid and uncomfortable with lavish meals and wasted food. With other students I used to help at a leprosy clinic – once I had got over my fear of touching someone with the illness. I learned much from the cheerfulness of the children and the humour of older people who were badly disfigured. I also learned, as I watched Christians, Muslims and Hindus together caring for the patients, that God's kingdom will only come when people of all faiths together work for peace, care for the needy and treasure the environment.

The Poem

Two hymns by George Matheson

There is a welcome and growing recognition of the importance of interfaith understanding both for social cohesion and world peace. The emphasis on the practical benefits of good interreligious relations may, however, obscure the spiritual significance of dialogue. Pioneers of the interfaith movement hoped that the coming together of religions would reveal deeper insight into the mystery of the Divine and bind believers together in a fellowship of faith.

This is clearly expressed in a poem by George Matheson, which was often sung as a hymn at All Faiths services arranged by the World Congress of Faiths. The third verse says of the various religions:

> Each sees one colour of thy rainbow-light,
> Each looks upon one tint and calls it heaven;
> Thou art the fullness of our partial sight;
> We are not perfect till we find the seven.

The hymn begins with the affirmation that God's love is mediated through every religion and the hymn recognises that each faith has a particular insight to share.

> Thine is the Roman's strength without his pride,
> Thine is the Greek's glad world without its graves,
> Thine is Judaea's law with love beside,
> The truth that censures and the grace that saves.

George Matheson (1842-1906) was the son of a Glasgow merchant. Despite practically losing his eyesight when he was 18, he did brilliantly in his studies at Edinburgh University and became a minister of the Church of Scotland, first at Inellan and later in Edinburgh. In 1890 he published *Sacred Songs* in which 'Gather us in' appears. He died at North Berwick.

His best-known hymn is 'O Love that wilt not let me go' which he wrote on the evening of 6 June 1882 – the evening of his sister's marriage – after the woman to whom he was engaged had told him that because of his blindness, she felt unable to go ahead with their marriage. He said of the hymn, 'It was the quickest bit of work I ever did . . . I had the impression rather of having it dictated to me.' This is another hymn that has deeply influenced me and even as in my search for better Christian–Jewish relations I have had my faith questioned by the cruelty and horror of the Holocaust, I have held on to the belief that the deepest meaning of the universe is a Love which promises 'that morn shall tearless be'.

Even though it is a tearjerker, it is the hymn I would like sung at my funeral, because I see the whole of life as a call to surrender myself to a Love that will never let me go and in whose depths there is the promise of 'life that shall endless be'.

> Gather us in, thou love that fillest all;
> Gather our rival faiths within thy fold.
> Rend each man's temple-veil and bid it fall,
> That we may know that thou hast been of old.
>   Gather us in.

Gather us in: we worship only thee;
In varied names we stretch a common hand;
In diverse forms a common soul we see;
In many ships we seek one spirit-land;
      Gather us in.

Each sees one colour of thy rainbow-light,
Each looks upon one tint and calls it heaven;
Thou art the fullness of our partial sight;
We are not perfect till we find the seven;
      Gather us in.

Thine is the mystic life great India craves,
Thine is the Parsee's sin-destroying beam,
Thine is the Buddhists' rest from tossing waves,
Thine is the empire of vast China's dream;
      Gather us in.

Thine is the Roman's strength without his pride,
Thine is the Greek's glad world without its graves,
Thine is Judaea's law with love beside,
The truth that censures and the grace that saves;
      Gather us in.

Some seek a Father in the heavens above,
Some ask a human image to adore,
Some crave a Spirit vast as life and love:
Within thy mansions we have all and more;
      Gather us in.

***

O Love that wilt not let me go,
I rest my weary soul in thee:
I give thee back the life I owe,
That in thine ocean depths its flow
May richer, fuller be.

O light that followest all my way,
I yield my flickering torch to thee:
My heart restores its borrowed ray,
That in thy sunshine's blaze its day
May brighter, fairer be.

O joy that seekest me through pain,
I cannot close my heart to thee:
I trace the rainbow through the rain,
And feel the promise is not vain,
That morn shall tearless be.

O cross that liftest up my head,
I dare not ask to fly from thee:
I lay in dust life's glory dead,
And from the ground there blossoms red
Life that shall endless be.

My Philosophy of Life

Jesus is at the heart of my philosophy of life. My mother was a devout Christian and I am never aware of not having believed in God, an awareness constantly renewed by the beauty of nature. Already as a teenager I was thinking about ordination but at college, for a time, discipleship became a duty. A sermon by Cuthbert Bardsley, then Bishop of Coventry, convinced me of Jesus' love and total acceptance of me, regardless of my fears and sins and failures. Clouds of self-doubt or worry about work undone easily hide the sunshine of his grace, but it has been the bedrock of my life, reinforced by the always generous and encouraging love of Mary.

My adult life has been a growing awareness of the 'wide embracing, wondrous love of God' – a line from a hymn sung at our wedding, which I used as a title for my first book of sermons. In parish life I quickly discovered how many people radiate that love. It is easiest to see it in small children, but I have been constantly surprised by the presence of Divine compassion among those who suffer, even those dying of cancer as I have sat by their bedside. I quickly discovered that God's love is not confined to Anglicans – Mary was a Methodist! – but in the sixties church rules, which we usually ignored, meant we could not receive communion together. Nor is that love confined to Christians and the wonderful friendships with people of many religions – and even with members of so-called cults – has been evidence of this. Increasingly, I have recognised the divine joy in all nature, which is one reason why I became a vegetarian.

But is love really the meaning of the universe? In India, I was aware of the degradation that poverty can cause and when I worked for the Council of Christians and Jews, almost everyday I was reminded of the horrors of the Holocaust. God in giving us freedom has not, I think, held back a reserve of power to right the wrong, but shares the suffering and speaks through the cries of the victims to our consciences. The future is genuinely open, which makes how we live of critical importance. As the Jewish philosopher Hans Jonas wrote, 'We literally hold in our faltering hands the future of the divine adventure.'[1]

The preciousness of life calls for reverence for all beings, the overcoming of man-made barriers, a total rejection of violence and war, special concern for the poor and all the oppressed, and the attempt, however falteringly, in personal relations to copy Jesus' way of forgiveness – for in both personal and communal relations, there is, as Desmond Tutu says, 'no future without forgiveness'.

I only begin to live by my philosophy of life whilst I recollect the wide embracing love of God. The cross is both a symbol of that love and of a calling to follow the way of Christ.

> A Man of sorrows, of toil and tears,
> An outcast man and lonely –
> But he looked on Me, and to endless years
> Him I must love, Him only.[2]

NEIL BROADBENT

Having worked in hospitals, a museum and a cathedral, Neil Broadbent was ordained an Anglican priest 22 years ago. He has worked in inner city poverty, in counselling, in prison and with many psychiatrists. Interested in how spiritual growth occurs, he has worked in the healing ministry for 16 years. For the past 10 years he has served as Director of Sozein – a Churches' Ministry of Healing Trust.

The Person
In diverse places and times, many are the people whose care and kindness have greatly influenced me. At Christ's Hospital, Horsham it was the Revd John Hall-Matthews and his wife Tricia. At York University it was Father Fabian Cowper OSB; at York Minster Canon Reggie Cant. For my time at the Queen's College, Birmingham and at Birmingham University, I am indebted to the Revd Drs Anthony Bird and Michael Wilson. If I must pick the one person who has had the most profound effect upon my life it has to be the Revd Dr Martin Israel.

At York University, suffering from pulmonary tuberculosis, de-personalisation and psychic overload, I turned down the post given me, of president-elect of the Christian Union. Rejected in return by three hundred co-religionists, the only Christian exposition I could relate to was Martin Israel's booklet *The Power of the Spirit in Everyday Living*. It was, for two years, the only writing that made plain, honest, deeply radical sense to me.

In the comedy film *When Harry Met Sally* there is that well-known scene wherein Sally fakes sexual excitement in a restaurant. When the waitress asks a lady at a nearby table what she would like, the customer, who cannot take her eyes off Sally, says 'I'll have what-ever she's having!' To this day I can adaptively echo her comment as I read or hear Martin's words.

Year upon year I have heard the very word of the Lord, for me, delivered through Martin's lips. On three occasions I was able to attend his Good Friday three-hour service of devotion at Holy Trinity Church, to the rear of the Royal Albert Hall. Each year his outwardly plain and inwardly divinised exposition of the seven last words of Christ would ascend to ever higher realms of commingled sorrow and glory to end, at the dot of 3 p.m., on a note beyond which no more could be said. It was a seeming aside in one such service that lead me to take up once again my other favourite mystical author – the Revd William Law.

One year, on a clergy retreat at the Franciscan house in Hemingford Grey, I was informally pouring out my abiding sins. In a comfy manner, reminiscent of wearing a pair of worn slippers, Dr Israel declared, 'You can't help it, Neil.' My faults of commission and omission were not belittled, far less ignored, yet in that moment my heart and soul were bathed in invisible warmth and I was made aware of the overwhelmingly self-evident truth that every part and particle of my being was totally and utterly cherished by infinite Love, also known as God.

His learning, great suffering and mystical experiences have led him to expound no 'pie in the sky when we die' fantasy of the state religion of our land but an unwavering message of 'Do what God requires of you today as revealed by your present circumstances.'

I long every day to be a priest of the most high God after the order, not of Melchizedek, but the Revd Dr Martin Israel.

The Book

The nature and action of love, the Christ of God, is laid out in the book which has most profoundly affected me: *The Spirit of Prayer & The Spirit of Love* by William Law (1686-1761).[1] It has transformed my reading of the New Jerusalem Bible and my understanding of Christianity and true spirituality.

In beautiful English, Law explains how divinisation may become a living reality now (cf. 1 John 4:16-18). Clear and simple classic prose sets forth, to my mind, irrefutable descriptions that are true to experience. In it the finest Christian mystic this land has produced writes,

> God, as considered in himself, in his holy being, before anything is brought out of him, is only an eternal will to all goodness. This is the one eternal, immutable God, that from eternity to eternity changes not. As certainly as he is the creator, so certainly he is the blesser of every created thing, and can give nothing but blessing, goodness and happiness from himself,

because he has in himself nothing else to give. It is much more possible for the sun to give out darkness than for God to do or be, or give out anything but blessing and goodness.

Love is the Christ of God. Wherever it comes, it comes as the blessing and happiness of every natural life, as the restorer of every lost perfection, a redeemer from all evil, a fulfiller of all righteousness, and a peace of God which passes all understanding . . . It comes down from heaven; it regenerates the soul from above; it blots out all transgressions; it takes from death its sting, from the devil his power, and from the serpent his poison. It heals all the infirmities of our earthly birth.

Christ given for us is neither more nor less than Christ given into us. He is in no other sense our full, perfect and sufficient atonement than as his nature and spirit are born and formed in us, which so purge us from our sins that we are thereby in him, and by him dwelling in us, become new creatures, having our conversation in heaven.

To have salvation from Christ is nothing else but to be made like him. It is to have his humility and meekness, his mortification and self-denial, his renunciation of the spirit, wisdom and honours of this world, his love of God, his desire of doing God's will and seeking only his honour.

Look not at pride only as an unbecoming temper; nor at humility only as a decent virtue; for the one is death and the other is life; the one is all hell and the other is all heaven.

We are strangers to heaven and without God in the world, for this reason only, that we are void of that spirit of prayer which alone can unite, and never fails to unite us with the one only Good, and to open heaven and the kingdom of God within us.

His writings are so powerful that I spent some five years researching the man and his wisdom, primarily for my own preaching, prayer and teaching. In print, there is a collection of the very best of William Law entitled *The Devout Life: William Law's Understanding of Divine Love*.[2]

The Place

I fled home at the age of ten. Much of my life has felt as if I was living out of a suitcase. The place, then, that has had the most profound effect upon me is my present home – even if it is living above the factory.

In November 1987, a small team moved in to the Old Vicarage. The house had great potential. The fifty centimetres of water in the cellar had room for more frogs and newts. The many hearths and disused chimneys showed scope for central heating. So the work began; recycling, repairing and restoring. We took inspiration from the rear view overlooking a beautiful valley of fields and trees – itself a reclaimed site of opencast coalmining.

Priorities had to be decided. The first room to be transformed became the prayer-room or chapel, in every sense the centre of the house. Out went the fireplace. In came gentle shades of blue, a couple of chairs and lots of prayers.

Come spring and new life came in the form of new windows and new help for the grounds. Cuttings were to be found on most window ledges and relationships were beginning to root in the village.

The front door area was underpinned. The hall floor was dug up; in some places to a depth of one and a half metres. The antique tile flooring, sadly, was replaced with a beautiful carpet. One chimney was taken down completely and the rest substantially repaired. The roof gully was rebuilt and waterproofed: no longer would melting snow lead to water running down the lighting flex by the airing cupboard. The front door would now open and the back door shut properly.

The team dwindled to one and, when it seemed the venture might fold, resurrection came – at the end point – in Easter 1993 when I married Barbara and the house was filled with three glorious teenagers.

And as it is with the building so it is for some of the visitors. 'Here,' as a trustee once said, 'people meet their real selves and discover what it is to love themselves and be loved by others and by God. By the gently strong work of the Spirit of God broken hearts are bound together, captives are released and people who feel themselves to be imprisoned are set free.'

Supported by a large team of helpers, many now friends, and an unseen cloud of witnesses, Sozein attracts folk who are dissatisfied with their fare; they may be physically, emotionally, mentally, psychically or spiritually dis-eased. Reconsidering one's life to date and reconnecting with the divine requires time, privacy and space to be quiet. As much attention as we can muster is paid to them for 'absolute, undivided attention is prayer' as Simone Weil wrote. A three-way conversation, often consisting of silence, is established between our guests, ourselves and our creator in the quiet expectation that good may emerge from their troubles, a veritable light in their darkness.

The Poem

I struggle greatly to understand virtually every form of poetry, so I have offered my favourite prose piece which I cannot but help read devotionally. The Revd Alan Watts wrote this in *Behold the Spirit*.[3]

> The meaning of the Incarnation, therefore, is simply that we do not have to *attain* union with God. Man does not have to climb to the infinite and become God, because, out of love, the infinite God descends to the finite and becomes man. Despite man's refusal of God, despite his pride, his fear, his helpless and hopeless involvement in the vicious circle of sin, God's nature remains unalterably love – the *agape* which consists in giving oneself wholly and without reservation to the beloved. Therefore the eternal Word, the Logos, becomes flesh, making our nature his nature; he assumes our limitations, suffers our pains and dies our death. More than this, he bears the burden of our sins: that is, he remains in union with us even though we crucify him and spit on him; he continues to dwell within us and to offer, or sacrifice, our lives to God even though we commit every imaginable form of depravity. In short, God has wedded himself to humanity, has united his divine essence with our inmost being 'for better for worse, for richer for poorer, in sickness and in health' for all eternity, even though we elect to be damned.
>
> > If I ascend up into heaven, thou art there;
> > If I make my bed in hell, behold, thou are there also.
>
> All that remains for us to do is to say, 'Yes–Amen' to this tremendous fact, and this is still within the power of our fallen nature. Our motive for saying it, however perverted by pride and fear, makes not the least difference, because the fact is the

fact: we have been given union with God whether we like it or not, want it or not, know it or not. Our flesh has become his flesh, and we cannot jump out of our own skins. And once we realize the futility of our pride, that we can neither ascend to God nor, by reason of pride, prevent his descent to us, the proud core of egoism is simply dissolved – overwhelmed by God's love. The function of Christian morality and spirituality is not to earn or deserve this gift of eternal life, but rather to appreciate and express it. The saint is holy not to attain union with God, but to give thanks for it.

Julian of Norwich wrote, similarly, that 'Our failings never hinder Him loving us.' William Law wrote in one of his *Letters to Clergy* of the necessity of surrendering oneself unconditionally; 'you are ... to give up yourself absolutely and entirely to God in Christ Jesus as into the hands of infinite Love'. Such thoughts encourage me to keep on offering to God not only my Sunday best but also my weekday worst, giving God time, in the silence, to love the hell out of me. When I explained to a nun that it had taken me thirty years to understand what the Christian faith was all about, she giggled and said, 'Now all you have to do, Neil, is live it.'

My Philosophy of Life

Offering Oneself as Servant

The following piece was given me in prayer on a train to London to supply an article for the parish magazine of St Peter's Church in Belper on my philosophy of life. A version of it is to be found in *Learning to Love* by Martin Israel with Neil Broadbent.[4]

The art of Christian service is the art of the three-way conversation. Skill in service, like any other skill, grows with practice. Being a group activity in which the participants are God, self and other(s), there are always present the openly acknowledged agenda and a hidden set of intentions and wishes. 'Our thoughts are not His thoughts and our ways are not His ways', as the prophet Isaiah declared long ago.

As the purpose of this life is that we may grow in love and usefulness to our neighbour, a prerequisite is inner knowledge of our own strengths and weaknesses. As we are to incarnate divine love and compassion in our souls and bodies, we need a continuing over-shadowing by the Holy Spirit that we may think only those thoughts that the Lord would have us think, speak only those words that God would have us express and do only those deeds that conform with his desire for our wholeness and holiness.

The Easter people are those who know the power of Christ and his resurrection because they have gone through their own Gethsemane, crucifixion and harrowing of their own inner hell and have been raised up by God to a new life based much less on con-forming to the powers of this world: social custom and expectations, group unspoken fears and resentments, etc. and much more on the Truth that sets us free.

'Every member ministry' is right; it always has been and is a necessary antidote to past overdoses of priestly authority. But it is only Christian service to the degree that every participant in the group expression has set aside self-concern, self-protection, self-aggrandisement and all fears of self (because sin is self-will) and has the purity of heart to will only that which God desires.

This may seem a theory, a theology too far. Beyond the likes of us. In practice it isn't.

The more inner freedom we have to pay attention to what is actually happening in us, around us, and in our community and other groupings, the more clearly we can see not only what is going on but God at work in us. And 'absolute undivided attention is prayer', wrote Simone Weil. To love God more dearly, see him more clearly, and follow him more nearly we need like pygmies to stand on the shoulders of giants who have gone before us; the great women and men of prayer in the churches' past.

Sharing in the communion of such saints we are strengthened inwardly in the struggle to reduce the power of the seven deadly sins in us. As we 'hear all, see all and say next to nowt', we are em-powered not with potentially self-inflating charismata but with the fruit of the Holy Spirit; love, joy, peace, patience, kindness, goodness, and so on.

Our service improves as, along with John the Baptist, Mary, Jesus and St Paul, we continue to pray 'Your will be done, O Lord, not mine' on earth as it is in heaven.

DAVID CLARK

David Clark was a Choral Exhibitioner at Gonville and Caius College, Cambridge where he read English and theology. He began his ministry with four years as a curate in Leigh, Lancashire, followed by two years as Precentor of Manchester Cathedral. In 1970 Norwich drew him to serve for fifteen years as parish priest and later full-time Industrial Chaplain where he was a co-founder of the St Martin's Housing Trust with its night shelter and other support for the homeless. He was also deeply involved in unemployment issues. In 1985 he became Team Rector of Oadby, Leicestershire. From there in 1998, unusually, he became a curate again, at St James the Greater, Leicester, in order to fulfil a call to make a contribution to interfaith relations in the city.

The Person

I could claim Sarah, my wife and best friend, as the greatest influence on my life. She has supported and accompanied me over forty years, from training at Wells Theological College, through successive career changes and shared decision-making in family life with our four children. But I cannot write about her now: the right words will not come.

So many others have shaped my path. One was Hugh Montefiore, who was Dean at Gonville and Caius College, Cambridge, and at a crucial point, tutor in New Testament studies. He kicked my intellectual backside for me. I was very ashamed of the lazy work I was producing at that time, but now, at last, I started to study. It was difficult for the queen of sciences, theology, to compete, as I was in love with music. At the end of a rich three years, in 1960, when I was 21, National Service had been abolished and I needed experience. The Dean said, 'Go to Africa!' I went to Nigeria and taught English and some French in Gbongan/Ode-Omu Anglican Grammar school for a tour of duty, arriving in time to haul down the British flag and salute Nigeria's independence.

Another influence was my Nigerian headmaster, Mr Adeniji, who helped me accept my inexperience and guided my first steps in teaching. This was an invaluable and formative experience. Living on campus with the staff and students, my nearest white neighbour 17 miles away, I learned acceptance and appreciation of difference. Now, forty-three years later, the Chief Rabbi has written an impressive book called *The Dignity of Difference* which is strongly addressed to the current situation in our globalised society. But its great wisdom contains understandings which I learned then.

Apart from a certain intellectual rigour, which I have never entirely been able to live up to, Hugh Montefiore gave me a breadth of vision. Himself a Jewish Christian, I could not avoid the uncomfortable feeling that the Christian Church never quite manages to be respectful and open about its Jewish roots. Today, with the clear connection between Christianity and the anti-Semitism which led to the Holocaust,[1] the need for the Church as a whole to revise its attitudes not only to Jews but to the other world faiths, becomes a profound necessity.

In a way it was Mahatma (Great Soul) Gandhi who clinched matters for me. When I read Nanda's biography in the seventies, I was astounded to discover that this man knew the Bible and could quote freely from it and yet remained a Hindu with Jain sympathies and a broad sympathy for other faiths as well. But also I was impressed by his commitment to non-violent direct action and by his practice of non-violence to pursue his campaigns for independence. For all his faults and, debatably, his political mistakes, he is indeed for me one of the great souls of the twentieth century. His calmness under pressure and his willingness to undergo racist attack are ideals which have inspired me over the years.

I am seldom the object of racist sentiments, though I know they exist. But I am aware of how much my friends in minority groups are attacked because I learn of it in various asides which they make. Our young and attractive Orthodox Rabbi was recently punched in the face in the city and the city's Muslims became noticeably more nervous after the attack on New York's twin towers of the World Trade Center on 11 September 2001. To face the threat of inter-communal violence, the Bishop of Leicester, Tim Stevens, regularly convenes the faith leaders to take the pulse of the city, aided by the police. Together, we affirm our commitment to each other and thus the leaders are able to head off incipient trouble – so far – and we live in hope.

Another person who helped give me new direction in the late nineties was Bede Griffiths. I was deeply moved by the biography by

Shirley du Boulay. His vision of the marriage of East and West (the title of one of his books[2]) and his complementarity of religious insight and spiritual practice animates me deeply.

The Book

When I consulted my friend Alan Race about this project he, ever the opportunist, advised me to choose *Christianity and Religious Pluralism* by Alan Race. But I didn't fall for that, despite acknowledging that it has influenced me greatly, if only in the last five years. There's really only one book which has influenced me throughout my life and that's the Bible. That's inevitable really because I read some verses from it at morning and evening prayer and study other passages more deeply whenever I have a sermon to preach or a thought to follow up. Having said that, since the Bible is a library rather than a book, what has greatly influenced me? Genesis, the Psalms, Isaiah, the minor prophets and the Gospels are the chief influences. And how can I choose this book, thought of as the exclusive property of the Jewish and Christian religions (of course it's not), when I am dedicated to interfaith work?

Traditionally, the Bible has been used to bolster up an exclusive view of Christianity. However, when I read about God setting his rainbow in the clouds as a sign of his covenant with Noah, I find:

> This is the sign of the covenant which I have established with all that lives on earth (Gen. 9:12).

This is God's covenant with *all that lives*, which includes the whole of humanity, the plant and the animal kingdoms. This implies a unity and interdependence of all living things, which we have never fully acknowledged, but which is present in the mystical understanding of the unity of all creation, testified to by Mystics of all ages.[3]

The famous text 'I am the Way, the Truth and the Life' complete with capital letters, is trotted out whenever I am in the environment of a particular 'Christian' tribe and I disclose that I go to Hindu temples, Muslim mosques and Sikh gurdwaras. The most sensible application of this text I have heard is that it is undoubtedly true that *for Christians* Jesus is the way and the truth and the life. But we have no business imposing that truth for us on people of other faiths when often for them it cannot apply. No theological colonisation!

I suppose my chief inspiration has been in the behaviour of Jesus. I think of his masterly inactivity faced with the Pharisees baying for the blood of the woman caught in adultery, then his telling words (John 8). Then there is his obedience to his inner vision of God and the Kingdom, his way with his followers and his determination in setting out for Jerusalem, and his dignity during the trial and crucifixion. These are imprinted upon me. This is the human face of God: a man who was inclusive and compassionate towards everyone.

The Place

The reconstructed cell of Mother Julian of Norwich in St Julian's Church, off Rouen Road in Norwich, became a centre of healing and renewal for me in 1981 after a breakdown which caused me to take six months' sick leave. I had discovered this haven of peace and meditative quiet in the centre of a busy city some years before and paid an occasional visit. But in 1981 I walked there daily across the centre of the city for an hour of emotional prayer accompanied by tears, the gift of tears. Earlier, Father Llewelyn had often been there when I entered the cell and with him I had learned to kneel perfectly still on the prayer stool and become quiet before God. This gave my life as an industrial chaplain some balance but it was not enough and when the breakdown came, the supportive quiet of this place swung a foundational calm beneath me to permit my anguished inner howling. In time I found healing.

When I came to leave Norwich in 1985 for a new post as Team Rector of Oadby, I was nervous about the new responsibilities and wondered aloud to a friend who met me one day in St Julian's whether I would be able to find another such pool of silence. 'It will be there waiting for you,' she said. And so it was, in the Lady Chapel of St Peter's, Oadby, where I meditated on most days in the early morning.

There, 13 years later, an extraordinary experience occurred in February. For several minutes it seemed as if a text was written in capital letters across my forehead, or impressed upon my brain with great insistence. The words were, 'Seek my face in the city'. I recognised the words from Psalm 27: 'You speak in my heart and say, "Seek my face": your face, Lord, will I seek.' I realised that I was being called to pray in the city. Many Christians feel unnecessarily a curious constraint about visiting the places of worship of other faiths. I felt the call was to use my willingness to operate outside the ecclesiastical limits, which I had learned as an industrial chaplain, and to make a contribution to relations between the faiths.

Here in Leicester I have been extremely fortunate that the then Bishop, Tom Butler, and Glynn Richerby, the vicar of the large city church of St James the Greater, allowed me to take a part-time post as Associate Priest where I began to explore an interfaith ministry in a multicultural context. At that time, the Bishop's interfaith adviser for Leicester was Dr Michael Ipgrave, now performing a similar function for the Archbishop of Canterbury and Churches Together in Great Britain and Ireland. I learned much from him.

Now, I live in the curate's house in a quiet backwater a few hundred yards from the church. My neighbours are Hindu, Sikh, Jewish, Muslim, as well as Christian. It is a truly multi-faith city, with seven Sikh gurdwaras, twenty-two mosques representing various Muslim traditions, eighteen Hindu temples, a Jain temple, two Buddhist viharas, two Jewish synagogues and the usual variety of Christian churches. These serve, according to the latest census figures, 41,248 Hindus, 33,885 Muslims, 11,796 Sikhs, 638 Buddhists, 417 Jews and 125,187 Christians. My heart has been warmed as I have met many people in all of these traditions and, although it should be obvious, I have slowly realised that the religion of these people informs their good behaviour, their morals, their family values, their prayer life, in just the same way as my religion informs mine. Their places of worship have become significant to them as they continue to be hallowed by prayer and meditation of great diversity.

The Poem

Although I scarcely understood them, I was drawn to the metaphysical poets in the sixth form. Years later I had recourse to them to feed my soul. I have selected four of the seven verses of the poem *The Flower* by George Herbert. Verses two and three especially expressed my feelings during and after the breakdown I have mentioned. George Herbert not only writes poems which may be sung and which have passed into our classical hymnody and anthem repertory, *Teach me, my God and King*, for example, but he penetrates the deep movements of the soul. Are we accepted by God? Can I really be acceptable? The fourth verse suggests an answer.

How fresh, O Lord, how sweet and clean
Are thy returns! ev'n as the flowers in spring;
To which, besides their own demean,[4]
The late-past frosts tributes of pleasure bring;
      Grief melts away
      Like snow in May,
As if there were no such cold thing.

Who would have thought my shrivel'd heart
Could have recover'd greennesse? It was gone
   Quite under ground: as flowers depart
To see their mother-root, when they have blown;
      Where they together
      All the hard weather,
Dead to the world, keep house unknown.

And now in age I bud again,
After so many deaths I live and write;
   I once more smell the dew and rain,
And relish versing: O my onely light,
      It cannot be
      That I am he
On whom thy tempests fell all night.

These are thy wonders, Lord of love,
To make us see we are but flowers that glide:
   Which when we once can find and prove,
Thou hast a garden for us, where to bide.
      Who would be more,
      Swelling through store,
    forfeit their Paradise by their pride.

To use the flower as an extended metaphor for the soul's life is quite brilliant. Through it, Herbert conveys fragility, the suffering of the soul, wonder, awe and praise. The first line reminds me how fortunate I am, while the last verse recalls me to humble gratitude.

My Philosophy of Life

I am nervous of claiming that I have a philosophy of life. That would imply that I had a philosophical mind, which thought coherently about things, like a friend of mine who makes logical connections and comes to profound conclusions while soaking in his bath. It would also imply that I had now wrestled with the implications of postmodernism, about which I remain extremely unclear.

I suppose I live by a series of insights gleaned from wide reading and experience. They include the following:

- I like to be outgoing but increasingly realise the necessity of withdrawal. As both industrial chaplain and interfaith navigator, I am sustained by Baron von Hügel's Germanic sentence: 'The lonely, new and daring (if but faithful, reverent and loving) outgoing of the discoverer and investigator are as truly acts of, are as necessary parts of, the Church and her life as his coming back to the Christian hive and community, which latter will then gradually test his contribution by tentative applications to its own life, and will in part assimilate, in part simply tolerate, in part finally reject it.'
- I hope I am generous in many ways, even though I make mistakes about the allocation of time. I am glad that circumstances have enabled me to be generous in an involvement with the other faith communities of Leicester.
- I try to practise humility and being willing to admit it when I am in the wrong. The term comes from the root *humus* – of the earth, earthy.
- I try to be honest – facing the facts even if it means getting it in the neck, such as when I've preached a sermon about feminism, racism, refugees and asylum seekers, or the immorality of the invasion of Iraq by Britain and America. In so doing I try to take care not to fall into stereotyping or prejudice myself.
- I am open to opportunity and spend a lot of time networking and providing people with cuttings and photocopies of things I know they will be helped by and interested in.

These insights help me seek the face of God, in the city of ethnic and faith diversity.

> O Lord, show me your true face
> And mine
> Before I die.
>   (From a prayer by Lama Surya Das)

JOHN DENNIS

John, now in his seventies, was a parish priest for twenty years, first in the East End of London on the Isle of Dogs and then in Mill Hill in north-west London. From 1979 he served a further twenty years initially as a suffragan and then as diocesan Bishop in Suffolk. He has always had a great interest in prayer, leads many retreats and undertakes spiritual direction. He is married to Dorothy whom he met when both were undergraduates in Cambridge. For the past 25 years he has been a Tertiary in the Franciscan Third Order. He has two sons, one of whom is a diplomat and the other a comedian, both skills he himself has needed frequently down the years.

The Person

It would be only right and fair to give this place to either my parents or my wife. If though it is to be someone beyond the immediate family, then I have no doubt at all whom I will choose.

When I was a boy in my early teens, my family was not a church-going family at all. When we went to see my grandparents in Yorkshire each summer for a few weeks during the school holidays we all went to church with them, but there was no suggestion of it in our London suburb during the rest of the year.

Then one spring day, 8 May 1945 – VE Day – when the war ceased in Europe, quite out of the blue my mother said to my father, 'Ronald, we ought to go to church on Sunday.'

I was 14 years old and really knew nothing of Christianity or churchgoing. My parents, I think, were in fact people of faith though my father had had his dented both by the trenches of the First World War and by his scientific background. (He was a school-master, teaching biology.) Their faith had lapsed and lain dormant for many years. (When I was evacuated during the phoney war in 1939–40, the children at the school I attended recited something together which I had never heard before. I realised much later that it was in fact the Lord's Prayer.)

My mother's suggestion therefore came as something of a surprise but we all went as she asked that Sunday and the next one and the one after that, until we were regular attenders. It didn't take long before my sister joined the Guides and I the Scouts. My elder sister by two years was more interested in church matters than I was and early in 1946, perhaps also as a result of peer pressure and leader pressure in the Guides, she said that she wanted to be confirmed. 'Right ho,' said my mother, 'then John had better be done at the same time.' I remember well that I didn't particularly want this. I wasn't sure that I believed in God at all and certainly I did not feel ready to take on the commitment which confirmation seemed to imply!

However, in those days boys of 14 still did what their mother said, so in due course I unwillingly went off to a confirmation class. I suspect that the reason why the vicar did not take these himself but farmed us out to an old retired priest who was living in the parish was probably because he was too busy to take us himself and the normal 'season' for his own confirmation classes was in another part of the year. The priest's name was Canon Holder. I never did know what his Christian name was or even his initial. I cannot tell you what he said. The list of topics covered in the classes has long since been forgotten.

It wasn't what he said, it was rather the person that he was that told its own convincing tale to me. A gentle, loving, elderly man, who certainly filled my mind for the first time with the intellectual realities of the Christian faith but who even more significantly filled my heart with a burning desire to be like him. He was, for me, the incarnation of what Christian faith and love and hope and joy looked like. By the end of his classes not only was I convinced of the reality of the Christian faith, I was also convinced that I was being called to the priesthood. It was a conviction which came early and stayed firm through all the following ten years to my ordination as deacon in 1956, as priest in 1957 and on into my ministry ever since.

If my mother hadn't been moved by the ending of the war to want to thank God for its ending; if my sister hadn't joined the Guides or wanted to be confirmed like the others, I wonder whether I would have heard my calling some other way. God doesn't let go of us so I suppose I would, somehow. But I am enormously grateful to Canon Holder for the part he did in fact play in it all. Sadly, I didn't ever tell him face to face or thank him but I comfort myself with the knowledge that he was probably told by others then and that certainly he will know now, having died very many years ago. I hope that he is pleased.

The Book

Of the writing of books there is no end. The reading of them is another matter. I sometimes wonder how often I, and other people, buy books because the review interests me and then never get round to reading them. They say that it is undoubtedly true that the Bible is the bestseller even now in this country. I doubt if it is the most widely read. For myself it certainly is the book of life, or rather the library of life, and I would most certainly want it on my desert island with priority over all others.

However I suspect that another answer is required. If that is so, then I would turn to some of the writings on spirituality which have nourished me. The contemplation of God, of the loving God, is for me the mainspring of my life. Prayer is not so much the *saying* of prayers, though they have their place, it is the *being* in his presence all the time and rejoicing in that reality, often saying or even thinking nothing but simply relaxing in him.

The book on love which has been a mainstay for me for many years and still nourishes me is therefore the one that I will choose: Mother Julian's *Revelations of Divine Love*.

This account of a series of insights shown to an unknown woman in Norwich, who was a recluse in St Julian's Church in the fourteenth century is rich and nourishing. Unknown for centuries following her death, they were rediscovered and published not much more than a century ago. In her years in the cell at St Julian's she gave much spiritual counsel to those who came to seek it from her. Her counsel must have been widely sought for her wisdom is compelling.

Her book is a spiritual document and its intention is to give help and counsel to those who desire to live in union with the God of Love. The centuries are effortlessly spanned and what she says is as appropriate for the twenty-first century as it was for the fifteenth.

> Many men and women believe that God is All-mighty and may
>   do all;
> and that He is wisdom and can do all,
> but that He is all Love and will do all,
> there they stop short.

She speaks of the 'courtesy of God'. Speaking of him, hers is the phrase: 'Love is my meaning'. She writes: 'He comforts readily and sweetly by His words and says "But all shall be well, all manner of thing shall be well." These words were shewed full tenderly.'

She is full of wise encouragement and reassurance and she is to be read and read many times, each time bringing deeper understanding. I could quote her far more extensively but far better it would be for others to pick her up themselves and perhaps even make her their own favourite book as well.

The Place

It fascinates me that as I grow older I increasingly want to go on pilgrimage, to visit the places which have been crucial to my past. I understand that this is not an infrequent desire. Perhaps it is a rounding off of life. Some places have recurred during my life – Suffolk or Winchester. Some have been critical for particular events – like Ripon Cathedral where I was ordained and over 20 years later welcomed as the suffragan Bishop, or York Minster where I was consecrated Bishop, or Southwark Cathedral where I was confirmed, or the Cambridge University Divinity School where I first set eyes on my wife to be, or All Saints Hall Church in Bury St Edmunds where we married, or RAF Calshot at the end of Southampton Water where I whiled away my time on national service. The list could be a long one.

However the place I would chiefly concentrate on, asked as I am to identify one, is a mining village in the South Yorkshire coalfield, as it was then. The village is Kiveton Park but it is adjacent to the much older village of Wales. Here it is that my father and my uncle were brought up. My father, who was no sort of cricketer (and neither am I), always used to say that had he been good enough he could have played cricket for Yorkshire even though he was born in Wales!

My grandfather, another John Dennis, was an intelligent and highly civilised man who spent his life working as a miner until ill health forced him out of the pit and he became caretaker of the village/church hall until he died of lung cancer. My grandmother was one of many children of a working-class family in Hull, who went into service in the vicarage of Wales church. She too had had little formal education but when she saw, in the vicarage children, how highly prized and highly influential a good education was, she was determined to seize it for her two sons. She was a determined Yorkshire woman who got her way in that as in many other things. My father and my uncle were among the first pupils of the newly opened grammar school three stations along the railway line from Kiveton Bridge Station. They both served as officers in the army in the First World War. My father subsequently took a degree and went into teaching. My uncle ended up as an education officer in the Royal Navy.

Kiveton/Wales for me was the home of my grandparents, both of whom I dearly loved. It was also the place where I was baptised in the ancient Norman font of Wales church. I was evacuated there, to my grandparents, during the second half of the London Blitz in 1940 after I had contracted typhoid fever and was convalescing. During that period I was sent to the local primary school among all the sons and daughters of the colliery workers and learned that to survive I had to merge, lose my 'posh' London accent and become a Yorkshire tyke. I can still do it, if sufficiently provoked! My grand-father died when I was still a boy. My grandmother lived to see me ordained as a deacon and spent Christmas with my wife Dorothy and myself in Leeds in the first year of our married life. She died later that winter in 1956. Both of my grandparents are buried in Wales churchyard and even now nearly fifty years later, whenever I am passing by (it is these days only a couple of miles from the M1) I will look in, say a prayer for them, drink in the memories, clear the grave and tidy it up and then move on refreshed.

As a place it seems on the surface hardly to have changed. The pit though is closed and the men have had to find work elsewhere. They are still that hardy Yorkshire stock and I am proud to have that strain in my blood too.

The Poem

Poetry has a remarkable gift for expressing beauty, sentiment, pain, joy, emotion. It is for me the economy of words, saying much in little which appeals. Gerard Manley Hopkins with his 'The world is charged with the grandeur of God'. Or Thomas Traherne, strictly speaking in prose, but with a poetic ear, 'I thought the corn was oriental and immortal wheat, which never had been sown nor ever should be reaped'. Or modern poets like David Scott in his wonderful short poem on prayer with the line 'love meeting Love before the house wakes up'. These all attract me.

However I have no doubt at all what for me is the poem which resonates and returns to mind and to heart again and again:

> Love bade me welcome: yet my soul drew back,
>   Guiltie of dust and sinne.
> But quick-ey'd Love, observing me grow slack
>   From my first entrance in,
> Drew nearer to me, sweetly questioning,
>   If I lack'd any thing.
>
> A guest, I answer'd, worthy to be here:
>   Love said, You shall be he.
> I the unkinde, ungratefull? Ah my deare,
>   I cannot look on thee.
> Love took my hand, and smiling did reply,
>   Who made the eyes but I?
>
> Truth Lord, but I have marr'd them: let my shame
>   Go where it doth deserve.
> And know you not, sayes Love, who bore the blame?
>   My deare, then I will serve.
> You must sit down, sayes Love, and taste my meat:
>   So I did sit and eat.

It is in one way a eucharistic poem and certainly as a eucharistic devotion it has enormous power. Strictly though it is poem about the last things – about God's love in the face of our weakness and about his promise of eternal life at that heavenly banquet to come. It is English coming from a period of great spiritual flowering in the seventeenth century. I love it and delight in it and pray it and believe it.

My Philosophy of Life

What else than to love God and to love all his children for his sake? To believe that he is active and present in his twenty-first-century world and to seek to discern his presence and activity, working with him rather than against him; to enjoy life in its richness as he intends that we should, and therefore to go forward in hope.

Bishop David Jenkins was once asked what his own personal 'credo' was and his reply:

> I believe in God
> I believe in God as he is in Jesus
> And so there is hope.

Amen to that.

DENIS DUNCAN

Denis Duncan is a minister of the Church of Scotland, who served in parishes in Kelso, Juniper Green (Edinburgh) and Glasgow. He was Editor of the national religious weekly newspaper *British Weekly* from 1959 to 1970 and continued to contribute to it until 1982. He was formerly Chairman/Director of the Highgate Counselling Centre, London, Director of Hampstead Counselling Service, Associate Director of Westminster Pastoral Foundation and Training Supervisor in their national organisation, Chairman of the World Association for Pastoral Care and Counselling and Director of The Churches' Council for Health and Healing. He is the author of eleven books and the editor of many more. He has written over 400 meditations for the Saturday edition of *The Daily Telegraph* over the past 12 years.

The Person

When the late and great Scottish preacher John White was asked in a radio programme what had led him to give his life to ministry and service, he replied simply and succinctly: 'I met a Man.' Those like myself who have spent a lifetime in such ministry and service will endorse his reference to Jesus Christ, but for the purpose of this book, I obviously have to name someone of lesser standing than that, but whose influence, nevertheless, has been of great importance to me.

Nearly 60 years of ministry implies many lasting relationships and brief encounters, the latter often as important as the former. I think for example of a very short meeting with Tojohiko Kagawa, of George MacLeod, of Major Alida Bosshardt, the Salvation Army officer who served for nearly 30 years in the red-light district of Amsterdam. I think, too, of Sister Frances Dominica, founder of Helen House in Oxford and now Douglas House too. The former is a hospice for seriously ill children, the latter for young people. There is too that circle of inspiration summed up in words like family, friends, partners.

Asked to tell of the person who has most influenced my life, I want to focus on one of the greatest biblical expositors of all time, Professor William Barclay. His reputation is worldwide, his books are legion and his influence continues long after he himself has journeyed on.

I knew Barclay the teacher, the preacher, the biblical expositor, the broadcaster, the scholar. Barclay wrote for, as he described him, 'the plain man'. He was a populariser by choice. His aim was to open the scriptures to the man-in-the-street and the woman-in-the-pew. His *Daily Study Bible*[1] is a monumental and on-going contribution to the understanding of the Bible. Blessed with a photographic memory, he could interpret the Bible through the written word with clarity and illumination. But he would do it too on radio, on television and wherever he was invited to go and preach.

My close association with William Barclay was much developed when I was Editor of the national religious weekly, *British Weekly*. To that journal he contributed a whole page – an expository article, a 'sermonette' (*Seen in the Passing*) and a major prayer, often on health and healing. All this material ultimately became books.

Barclay's influence was great in many ways. I mention four particular qualities I admired:

- His use of time: Barclay was stone deaf. When he wanted to write (which was very often) he simply switched off the very visible hearing-aid he wore and no one could disturb him. Between teaching his classes in Trinity College in the University of Glasgow, he would retreat to his retiring room and those passing by would hear his typewriter going merrily. On his daily journey between his home and Glasgow University he used his bus ride to read many books. Never a minute was lost. That made its mark on me.
- His Scottishness: Barclay lived in industrial regions like Motherwell, Renfrew and Glasgow. He was therefore a man of the people, down to earth, indeed earthy (he had his human failings). His voice was rugged and always recognisable. He stayed in touch with the plain man and woman and understood them.
- His legendary generosity (as I had cause to know): With a mass of books published, royalties came from many directions but he was virtually uninterested in money. That kind of man makes an impression on you.
- His genuine humility: A huge intellect, a man of encyclopaedic knowledge and of the highest professional standing, he remained forever humble. How can one fail to be influenced by a man like that?

The Book

'Small is beautiful.' Small indeed is the book which has done so much to shape my life and see the direction in which it should go. I am referring to *The Forgotten Talent*[2] by Cameron Peddie.

It is clear that the disciples had understood the implication of Jesus' twin commands – to preach the gospel and to heal the sick. Hauled before the authorities to explain in what name they had carried out the healing of the crippled beggar outside the temple, they were told not to continue to heal in the name of Jesus. Praying for strength to 'obey God rather than men', they said: 'Help us to preach the Word with boldness by stretching out your hand to heal, signs and wonders following.' From early in my ministry, I felt called to hold preaching and healing together.

It was to observe the ministry of healing in action that I went, with Cameron Peddie's permission, to his healing sanctuary in the Gorbals district of Glasgow. Peddie had been called to be minister of that then notorious parish in the days of rival gangs. He approached his work from a social service point of view but came to see that something much more dynamic was needed. He realised it was the forgotten talent, the healing ministry of Jesus. It was in *The Forgotten Talent* that he told the story of his preparation for this ministry – spending the time between 11 p.m. and midnight in prayer every night for a year – and putting that ministry into action. It was a great and moving story. Every week Cameron Peddie would hold healing sessions in his sanctuary, a small hall in his church. To those sessions many came to receive his ministry. It was one of these occasions I went to observe.

I was sitting in the room watching him lay hands on (as he described it) 'the affected part' – heart, leg, chest, etc. He would ask those to whom he ministered if they felt heat or cold. Suddenly and without any warning he came across to me and said: 'Denis, there are too many people for me to deal with alone. Take the other chair and minister to some of them.' There was no time or space to consider the matter. I took the other chair, did what I had seen him do, asked the questions I had heard him ask. I was involved in healing ministry.

It was through *The Forgotten Talent* that I began to understand more about this ministry and its implications. It was the beginning of long-term participation in healing services which I have held continuously for thirty years and more. The influence of Cameron Peddie and his book could not have been greater.

The Place

It was the morning after we had arrived in Tiberias in the north of Israel. I went out and with a sense of wonder looked down on the Sea of Galilee below. Here was I on the hills above Tiberias and there was the water on which Jesus had walked, the lake on which he had calmed the storm ... and the disciples! Tiberias has left its mark on me in that it brought alive what had been, until then, simply the gospel story.

The island of Tresco in the Scillies is a quiet and peaceful place, cars being forbidden on the island. Walks along the cliffs or beach are largely solitary. The birds have their own sanctuary. The beautiful Abbey Gardens are world-famous. Tresco is a place that speaks of rest and relaxation, of rugged beauty and natural charm. There is a sense of closeness to nature and distance from the stresses of city life. Just because of all this, and the opportunity of companionship within its peaceful ways, the island has been an influence indeed.

However, as the place which has most influenced my life, I have chosen Amulree. It is a very small village just north of the Sma' Glen, on the road from Crieff to Aberfeldy. There is in Amulree a church, a hotel and a few houses, but that is all.

Although Amulree is a place of natural if wild beauty, nestling as it does among the hills and lochs of Perthshire, its importance is symbolic rather than literal. For one who has lived in cities virtually all his life – Edinburgh, Glasgow and, for the last thirty years, London – it represents calm, serenity, stillness and peace. But its significance is more than that. It happens to be, geographically, the centre of Scotland and so reflects to me the importance of my Scottish roots. Roots matter, especially theological roots, that is the faith in which one has been nurtured. When I wrote my devotional paperbacks, first *Creative Silence*, then *A Day at a Time*, followed by *Love, the Word that Heals*, I called the series *Amulree Paperbacks*. When I considered setting up some kind of network of prayer that would deepen the spiritual life of those who would be part of it, I called it the *Amulree Movement*. Its aims were the development of the emotional life, healing and reconciliation, the spiritual aspect of counselling, the meaning of wholeness. Circumstances prevented the full fashioning of that movement but its having Amulree as its name testified to the source and focus of its inspiration.

The needs of the soul must be nourished. Balance and harmony must be part of our being. Only so can we travel in the right direction, with the proper focus, with appropriate dedication. If our ways are to be ways of pleasantness and all our paths to be of peace, we need the memory of places like Tiberias and Tresco, and we need too the symbol of Amulree to nourish our deep roots and firm up our foundations.

The Poem

The poem that has most influenced my life must be one that has touched the heart of conviction and belief. For that reason I have nominated John Donne's *A Hymn to God the Father*.

Coming as I do from a background in Reformation theology and particularly the work of John Calvin, a major theme in my ministry has been the fact and nature of divine grace. Salvation is not a reward for good works, nor is it gained by merit or effort. It is a gift to be graciously received. The need for the gift of 'amazing grace' lies in the sinful nature of human beings. If the words 'original sin' seem out of date and irrelevant to modern people, so be it, but the factor they describe is a real one. Long ago, I heard the American theologian Reinhold Niebuhr give a seven-minute after-dinner speech in which he gave the most profound and searching analysis of the human dilemma. He said in essence that no man-made discipline, be it education, science, philosophy or anything else, could reach the depths of the human condition. Only the grace of God in Christ could reach that fundamental need. It is that sense of need and response which John Donne agonisingly reflects in his poem:

> Wilt Thou forgive that sin where I begun,
>> Which was my sin, though it were done before?
> Wilt thou forgive that sin; through which I run,
>> And do run still, though still I do deplore?
>>> When Thou has done, Thou has not done,
>>>> For I have more.

Wilt Thou forgive that sin which I have won
    Others to sin? and made my sin their door?
Wilt Thou forgive that sin which I did shun
    A year, or two: but wallowed in, a score?
        When Thou has done, Thou has not done,
        For I have more.

I have a sin of fear, that when I have spun
    My last thread, I shall perish on the shore;
Swear by thy self, that at my death thy son
    Shall shine as he shines now, and heretofore.
        And, having done that, Thou has done.
        I fear no more.

My Philosophy of Life

I believe in 'creative irresponsibility'. Let me explain what I mean by that phrase.

Having an attitude of responsibility, 'being responsible' in all things, is a proper and necessary endeavour but it can lead to a lifestyle and approach that is somewhat dull and even boring. On the other hand, sheer irresponsibility is indefensible. But there is something that lies between 'being responsible' and 'sheer irresponsibility'. It is an attitude of creative irresponsibility. In discussing a proposed project which nine out of ten people might well say cannot be done, perhaps on financial grounds, possibly practical grounds, the tenth person believes in that project, recognises the inherent difficulties but says it must be undertaken. The trouble is that the tenth person, though insisting that the plan must be carried through, cannot exactly say how it will be done. Just there lies the element of irresponsibility. What drives him or her on, despite the difficulties to be resolved, is the fact that the result when (not if) it is achieved will be highly creative.

Having always acted on this principle, let me give an example. A total of £500,000 needs to be raised to build a holiday house for severely disabled people and their families or carers. I have a responsibility for that. Already, through such an act of creative irresponsibility, a first house was built and fully equipped at a cost of £170,000 in Norfolk. It is in full use today. That a very small Trust in which I am involved and is led by a cerebral-palsied and blind woman, Lin Berwick, who is a wheelchair user, dares embark on such a huge project has been seen by many to be irresponsible but it will be an enormously creative project and it will be done.[3] This philosophy of life is not however whim or fancy. It is solidly rooted in basic convictions that are tried and tested.

The first of these convictions is a belief in an overruling providence. I never cease to be amazed at the workings of providence. Mistakes are made, sins committed, wrong directions taken, but still the jigsaw is pieced together. The omnipotence of God is wholly expressed in the divine ability to take even 'the evil that men do' and use it for right ends. *The second conviction* rests on the doctrine of forgiveness. It is that which constantly provides the opportunity to begin again, however badly things have gone wrong. I have said something about this in my choice of a life-influencing poem in the fourth gold ring. *The third conviction* relates to the fact that, whatever happened in the life of Jesus on Calvary and in the garden of the resurrection, 'it was for us he hung and suffered there'. Some will interpret those words as an atonement and think in terms of a 'substitutionary sacrifice'. I prefer to think of an 'at-one-ment', the renewing of a right relationship with God, neighbours, self and earth. *The fourth is a conviction* about healing which has been expounded in the second gold ring. God wants our wholeness in body, mind, soul and spirit.

Life is ultimately about direction, perspective, focus and dedication:

> **direction** – 'keep looking unto Jesus'
> **perspective** – 'seek first the Kingdom of God'
> **focus** – 'I know whom I have believed'
> **dedication** – 'follow me'.

Risk and adventure are part of the journey of which the theme, the essence of my philosophy of life, is 'creative irresponsibility'.

LAURENCE FREEMAN

Educated by the Benedictines, Laurence Freeman took a Masters degree in English literature at New College, Oxford. After some experience working at the United Nations, in merchant banking and journalism he entered Ealing Abbey as a Benedictine monk. After studying with Dom John Main in the novitiate and helping him with the establishment of the first Christian Meditation Centre in London in 1975, Father Laurence accompanied him to Canada where they had been invited by the Archbishop of Montreal to establish a small Benedictine community teaching and practising meditation. From here began the expansion of this spiritual tradition around the world. Father Laurence was ordained in 1980. After John Main's death in 1982, Father Laurence succeeded him and since then has been travelling widely to continue the work they initiated. When The World Community for Christian Meditation was formed in 1991, Father Laurence became its spiritual guide. Now based in London, he is a monk of the Monastery of Christ the King, Cockfosters. From the International Centre of the WCCM in London he serves a worldwide network of meditation groups; he is also active in the contemplative meeting of the different faiths and led the 'Way of Peace' initiative with His Holiness the Dalai Lama. His latest book is *Jesus, the Teacher Within* (Continuum, 2001).

The Person

I first met John Main when I was a boy at school. Our class was eagerly awaiting the debut of our new religion teacher, a monk, we were told, but not yet a priest. This made him seem an even easier prey than the previous teacher we had easily dispatched. As soon as he entered the room, however, we knew we had met our match. He had a self-evident authority and genuine ease of self-assurance. This was to bring out the best in us. He treated us as adults but never forgot we were children and the gap between these two levels was humour and a touch of Irish caprice with which he confused our Englishness. I cannot say why I remember that first encounter so vividly except that future events cast their shadow before them. I think it was recognition at a level deeper than reason or emotion of a person who would later give my life specific depth and direction. In the East it is a more common experience, the recognition of your guru.

My only other encounters with John Main during my school years were occasions when my rebellious spirit ran against the rules of the institution and he had to restrain my self-will. But it was some years later when I was at university and in a personal crisis that I appealed to him for counsel and he responded immediately and generously with time and attention. I did not realise then that he had just started to meditate again. With the lightest touch he dropped the seed of the practice into my confused and agitated mind. As a teacher he had both insight into people and a graced sense of timing as well as the patience to leave the rest to nature and to God. Which is what he did for the next few years.

I was drawn back to him when he started a lay community at his monastery in London. He was not over-encouraging about my joining but when I did it proved to be the turning point or rather the end of my career. My six months there under his guidance and kindness were a painful but liberating time of growth. It was an extraordinary gift and I could not say today how things would have turned out for me without it. In John Main I found a desert father in the suburbs of London. I hardly knew what it was that I was looking for or needed. But the terms became ever clearer. The ancient unspoken contract of the desert was the abba's fidelity to the disciple and the disciple's total openness with the teacher. It is a rare and powerful combination and while it works a glimpse of heaven is attained. It is also the cure of the soul.

I never felt as others did that his personality was overwhelming. We shared many interests and the same sense of humour. For me his personality was energising, visionary and liberating. Through all my struggles and ego-storms he never imposed his will or diminished my freedom to determine myself – even when it would have been easier for me to have been told what to do. Working with him on setting up the first Christian Meditation Centre and an attempt at a new kind of Benedictine community demanded of me and others what he always provided the opportunity for, total commitment. It was my training with him.

His degree of detachment, from people and his own achievements, was often hidden behind his intense commitment to everything he was engaged in. Maybe it needed to be hidden because detachment of that purity is frightening and easily misunderstood by those still attached to many things. With time I learned that his detachment was the basis of his extraordinary capacity to love. Love was his theology ('it's the only morality', he would say) and his practice. Meditation for him was simply exposure to love at its source.

His death metamorphosed the intense joyfulness and security of his presence into a vast silence and stillness. At first a wasteland, it became increasingly a desert that bloomed. I learned to trust his reassurance to me before he died and though I cannot see him I have felt only increasingly guided and protected by his spirit through all the mistakes I have made since being deprived of his immediate wisdom.

John Main occupies a place in my life and identity undiminished by time and strangely strengthened by death. Or rather he is a central place there. He is, as all truly influential people in our lives are, a junction in the network of our relationships. His presence empowered the expansion of that network towards the range of the infinite of which the soul is truly capable – as he knew and taught. His deep and solitary detachment was the human space in which Christ the true teacher, the centre of every centre, really began to be formed in me.

It is not false to say that I wish I could have been a better disciple even though the time was short. It is a measure of how I value his stature as my friend and teacher and as one who I am delighted to see has become a contemporary teacher for so many others.

The Book

I am tempted to choose *The Pickwick Papers*, a comic novel by Charles Dickens. It taught me at an early reading age that books can make you shake with laughter and that was to learn that books really matter. They are ways in which solitudes converse. Mr Pickwick's stodgy English decency, a Victorian Captain Mainwaring perhaps, Sam Weller the cocky Cockney, Pickwick's dull but loyal companions, like the slow-witted apostles, the fat boy's narcolepsy, Mr Pickwick's trial and imprisonment, transmuting Dickens' own childhood traumas into comedy. But it may not be the real gold ring because when I reread it, hoping to rediscover the first delight, it seems heavier going. But I feel the gratitude one always feels for books that awakened something for the first time.

I am also tempted to award, among many Shakespeare nominees, the gold to *The Winter's Tale*. Like all his comedies it is Mozart in words. The happy ending is not an evasion of life's tragedies, irreversible hurts, harm done to others, opportunities missed and time wasted. But it is a declaration of hope – the hope that is the spirit of art – that forgiveness and mercy bridge the 'wide gap of time'. All *will* be well. The last scene in which Leontes discovers Hermione's statue to be in fact her living self has such a reverence for the creative power of the divine in human affairs that you wonder if Shakespeare himself was only human.

The more I resist these temptations the more I find, so I had better get on and decide. The book that has most influenced me and continues to do so is the book of the gospels. The friendship of *The Pickwick Papers* or the redemption of *The Winter's Tale* are reflections of these themes from the gospels where they reside as archetypes. The book of the gospels achieves what every good book aspires to, complete authenticity. Significantly, this is at the price of the author's identity. Who were Matthew, Mark, Luke and John? Their personality, like that of St Benedict, was subsumed in their text.

More mysteriously, the central character of the gospel narratives has become the book that was written about him. If the Word became flesh, flesh also became word. Lacking obvious literary artifice they are still densely cross-referential, compacted with layers of meaning and great tracts of significant silence. Translation distances them from us, as does the commitment of any oral tradition to writing, yet that very distance becomes the space which real presence indwells.

The gospels are as quickly responsive to present mood as, say, the *I Ching*. It is as if they have an independent intelligence. Yet in the gospels it is always resolving into an intimate and knowable personal presence, a human closeness that respects the solitude that is our uniqueness.

Any book I read is set against the gospels' standard of seriousness, humility, conciseness and authenticity. They tell us why we are bothering to speak truthfully at all. Of the four gospels John is the glory, the most mystical and most human. In John especially we imagine or see Jesus laughing and weeping. Within John it is the resurrection appearances that make me feel that this book, although it may not have been the last book to be written, will be the last to be understood.

The Place

When I went to New College, Oxford for my interview, I fell in love with the place. Which perhaps means I objectively saw or felt something there I had not earlier recognised in myself.

What was it? The dons, students, college servants, have come, stayed, gone down or retired since the fourteenth century. A river is more than the water flowing through it. Beloved if mocked customs, worn steps, the smell of old libraries, intense arguments about things you know won't change much because only history not individuals defeat tradition, a class system in which the lower levels are the more snobbish, a rhythm of life that absorbs everything, the warmth and security of friendship.

The college and university are more than an institution. Institutions are about money and politics and they are there to *do* something. Organisms are about a life lived and aiming, however imperfectly, at perfection. It was this life in New College that captivated me at first sight, as the light in a rather plain person's eyes can make them more attractive than someone with better features. This life seemed to shape the buildings, the magical walled garden with the central mound where George Eliot once glimpsed the transcendent ideal of friendship, the chapel that sails through history, the monastic cloister that is the hidden heart of the place, too sacred for the agnostic English really to revere. It is not a museum, though. Epstein's modern Lazarus in the chapel, dodgem cars in the cloister, Monty Python in the television room, friends smuggled in or out of college after hours. The *place* is comprehensive.

The idea that all this was at the service of – what? Culture, education, ideas, civilised consciousness? This fascinated and overpowered me. It helped me accept something in myself I had not grasped before. The pettiness of academia or the decadence of students, which no member of college can or should entirely avoid, does not diminish the nobility of the endeavour, the 'idea of a university'. Clever students having fun, trying out their new personalities, discovering their desires, only seemed to make the idea richer. The college was the temple and the members its priests. But what was their god?

One night, standing on a ladder in the library, finding a book on mysticism I got a revelation. It was Pascal's *Memento*, the brief allusive record he sewed into the lining of his jacket and that captured some minutes' transformative experience of the presence of God. The final word of the *Memento* thrilled me and almost made me fall off the ladder. It started a clock ticking in me and although I was not very religious at university my spiritual path started there. The word was 'certainty'.

Jane Austen said you do not love a place the less because you suffered in it. When I go back to New College I pass the telephone box where I heard of my sister's death. I remember in the garden or the quad friendships, loves sought, found or lost. The place as an institution does not recognise me any more. Once it even did not want to let me in. But as an organism it remembers me better than I do myself. Which is perhaps why I like to take friends there who I want to share myself with.

Later I realised what it was I fell in love with on that first visit. It was the ideal of a monastery where the god of the place is actually acknowledged. A place which you enter to find something greater than space, boundlessness. A community in which you find more than the human form of love. A tradition that bumps you into true contemplation, the present moment.

Each time I return to New College it seems further away. Maybe that's time's effect on any ideal. As I was waiting for my admission result I had a dream of walking in some hills and seeing in the far distance a lovely city glowing in a golden light. For a while, and so in a sense for life, Oxford was that city for me. The dream recurs occasionally, sometimes in real life, especially when an epiphany is about to happen or to close. Where the real city, the New Jerusalem, is to be found is the question and the journey that New College helped me to get started on.

The Poem

When I was at Oxford a friend also studying English asked me if I had read George Herbert's poem *The Flower*. When I said no he looked amazed and said 'the greatest poem in the language' and walked off leaving me feeling very inferior. When I did read the poem I loved it and it might have been a gold ring had it not been for these circumstances. However it led me to Herbert's poem *Love (III)*: 'Love bade me welcome ... ' It becomes more gold on each reading.

It is a poem of infinite tenderness, not less than the divine unconditional love. But it is set against a background of bitter, self-induced suffering: 'Let my shame go where it doth deserve.' The struggle between God and ego is fiercer than that between flesh and spirit. One may hardly notice the darkness in the poem, as the light is so much stronger. Here divine compassion is confronted with human hard-heartedness and the resistance caused by self-hatred. It is human consciousness at the interface with its source and saying no.

Simone Weil turned the poem into a mantra by constant repetition and it taught her the mysteries of prayer. Perhaps it gave her her insight that God is like a beggar who keeps returning, waiting for our acceptance. Herbert had clearly also penetrated into this core Christian truth about the nature of God, so clear in the gospels and so difficult for people to believe.

Love in Herbert's poem, as in Shakespeare's sonnet, is an ever-fixed mark that 'alters not when it alteration finds'. It returns every shot of attempted rejection that we play with an effortless and, as Herbert notices, a smiling certainty and gentleness. The resistant ego plays its last card by hiding behind the mask of its sinfulness and presumes to tell God that it is not worthy of the divine hospitality: 'I the unkind, ungrateful?' Love plays its trump card when it reminds the soul of who created it. Even after its surrender, however, the ego tries to remain independent by assuming the role of a servant: 'My dear, then I will serve.' As Peter refused to have his feet washed. Love defeats this too – it is the tyranny of love – by insisting on being the one who does the serving. No one who understood this could turn the Eucharist into ecclesiastical politics.

The I's last word is 'So I did sit and eat'. The I and Love are united. Poetry is over.

My Philosophy of Life

I don't know if I have a philosophy of life. Most places I visit I could imagine spending a lifetime there and there are many philosophies and beliefs that I feel very happy inhabiting. Leaving one for another may be painful but it does not seem to me like rejection.

However I do have a preferred way of life and the best expression of its ideal is the Rule of St Benedict. The St Benedict of the sixth century may not have approved of the amount of time I spend travelling outside the monastery. But I think the Benedict of this century would understand and see the value of a monastery without walls. Fifteen hundred years ago the monk was characterised by renunciation. Today the challenge of a secular world is integration. The two approaches are not as contradictory as they appear and most situations demand a measure of both. We always have to let go but we also have to connect.

The timeless wisdom and adaptability of the Rule is its sense of measure, moderation, in all things. Many old pictures of St Benedict show him holding an object which some monks identify as a rod needed for correction. But others, I think the truer disciples, see it as a kind of metronome, a way of measuring the rhythms of life.

Prayer, work and study correspond in his vision to the tripartite harmony of the human person which is spirit, body and mind. They are indivisible yet distinct, interweaving yet autonomous. The anxiety and violence of much modern life arises from their being arhythmic and unbalanced. This is most critically seen in the problem of stress that is so destructive and yet is often not much more than the failure to measure out time properly and to respect one's whole self. Benedict appeals to today's business managers not only because he knows how groups work (or fail to) but also because he knows how to organise time. Discipline is the precondition of freedom and freedom is more than the ability to choose (as the modern consumer is persuaded). Freedom is the ability to consent to truth. And perhaps to dance in a pattern.

Time has turned the Rule into more of a poem than a rulebook. Benedict's vision, however, is expressed in very prosaic examples. It is all about balance in daily life leading to peace of soul and thus to a just society. But beyond this ideal is the ultimate goal, the meaning of human life. Benedict does not describe this in theological detail. He is quite zen-like in preferring practice to theory. He is not at all other-worldly. But he sees how, especially through love and friendship, the goal is already present in the journey itself. This I would say is the Christian philosophy, if philosophy is the right word, that I subscribe to.

JOYCE HUGGETT

Having graduated in history and theology from Southampton University in 1959, in 1960 Joyce began her first teaching post with severely deaf children; in 1974 she embarked on counsellor training and became Advisor to the Chinese Church of Nottingham. In 1986 her award-winning book *Listening to God* was published. This led to training in spiritual direction and retreat giving together with further writing on spirituality; later she and her husband David became mission partners with Interserve. They both moved to Cyprus where they established retreat facilities for missionaries and travelled extensively, leading retreats and providing pastoral care for missionaries throughout the Middle East and in other countries in the 10/40 Window.[1] They returned to England in 1998 and extended their home so that retreat work with mission partners could continue.

The Person

I was an undergraduate and he was a postgraduate engrossed in the world of aeronautics and space technology. Since I often saw him poring over Bible commentaries as well as the biblical text and since I respected this leader of the Christian Union, when my eccentric theology tutor fed me with teaching that seemed to clash with the beliefs on which I had been nurtured, it was to David that I took my qualms and my questions.

Romance with David at that time never entered my head. Three years later, though, just before I received my first degree and David received his doctorate, we got engaged. When we drove from our honeymoon to our first home, a door swung open for me, not only into an unfamiliar house but to an entirely new way of life. Life had revolved around the two-up, two-down Victorian terraced dwelling where I lived with my parents during the vacation and the hall of residence where I lived in term time. Now I found myself living in a gracious part of suburbia.

Comparing my childhood environment with Surrey still prompts me to ask: 'How did I make the transition?' I know the answer: it was David's gentleness that influenced me and eased me into this new way of life.

In the weeks between our honeymoon and term time when

David would resume his lecturing and I would begin teaching deaf children, we had fun making this home *ours*. My parents' home had no garden – only a back yard – so gardening was a foreign language for me. My parents' home boasted floors laid with lino not carpets so I had never used a hoover. David taught me how to use one. I could have felt hopelessly lost, lonely and inferior. Instead, David's acceptance of me was like sun shining on a water lily.

During these halcyon days, I not only blossomed, my world vision expanded as I attended lectures David gave. I would listen enthralled as through slides and lectures he opened people's eyes to the greatness of the galaxy and the wonder world of other planets. In those days I had never heard the phrase 'finding God in all things' yet through David's lectures, I found God in the wonder of space and marvelled.

'I realise I've reached a cross-roads,' David admitted two years after we were married. 'I have to choose between climbing the career ladder or pursuing a sense of calling – to seek ordination.' He was preparing for a lecture tour of Sweden at the time. While he was away, I sensed that he *should* test this call but wondered whether he could face the wrench of leaving this home, the affirmation that he was receiving and the success he was enjoying as a lecturer.

He returned in the full flush of a successful teaching tour. He also returned wanting to test his vocation. I marvelled at the way he made the necessary sacrifices – setting an example for me as well as incarnating the immortal words of Dag Hammarskjöld:

> For all that has been THANKS
> For all that will be YES.

The Place

Ten years later, having lived in Bristol where David trained for the ordained ministry and in Poole and Cambridge where he served his curacies, we moved to Nottingham – a place that was to expose me to previously unknown challenges and resources.

Here, a childhood dream was realised. I had always wanted to be a missionary. To my amazement, I discovered that the Chinese Church of Nottingham worshipped weekly in the church hall that 'happened' to be in our garden. This group welcomed me, invited me to speak at their meetings and looked to me as their 'pastor'. The friendships forged were deep, lasting, fun and resulted in many hilarious and happy cross-cultural family celebrations.

In Nottingham, too, I was expected to lead the Women's Fellowship: a group of women who met each Monday afternoon and whose prayers were the powerhouse of the then struggling church. The love, support and affirmation these women lavished on me enabled me to grow into a leadership role for which I felt ill-equipped.

Since the label 'Rector's Wife' also seemed to suggest to members of the church that I was competent to counsel them through many of life's crises, I took advantage of one of the many resources that Nottingham offered: the opportunity to train in counselling at St John's College.

St John's was just one of the colleges with which we forged close connections. Students gradually gravitated toward our city centre church and enriched our lives. The chaplain of one college invited David and me to speak on prayer at their annual retreat. The retreat was held in a nearby monastery. One of the monks sat in on our talks, befriended us over tea and invited us to return to make a retreat for ourselves. We did. The winsomeness of the plainsong, the profound sense of the presence and love of God in this prayer-saturated place acted on me like a magnet – drawing me back time and time again.

The chaplain at Nottingham University was an Anglican nun. Discerning what God was doing in my life, she invited me to make a retreat in her convent during her summer vacation. I did. Here I prayed in silence with the Sisters for an hour before breakfast. Here I was introduced to Robert Llewelyn's persuasive teaching on prayer. Here I discovered that the kind of prayer into which I was being drawn had a name: contemplative prayer. Here I started the first chapter of the rest of my life.

On my return from the convent a friend lent me a book, *A Method of Contemplative Prayer*. In this book, the author[2] claims that contemplative prayer and charismatic prayer spring from the same source: the Holy Spirit. This insight amazed me. This was the 1970s when many Christians worldwide were relishing renewal. While most expressed their new-found joy with exuberance, mine was being expressed in silent adoration. Jim Borst's book and the friend who lent it to me not only validated my journey but modelled the balanced spirituality that I coveted. They were two more of Nottingham's gifts to me.

The Poem

Jim Borst begins his book by describing contemplative prayer as a search for peace and a place of rest deep within ourselves where we rest and relax in his presence. This explanation reminded me of a poem that had drawn me to itself while I was on the retreat at the Anglican convent:

> Love bade me welcome: yet my soul drew back,
>   Guiltie of dust and sinne.
> But quick-ey'd Love, observing me grow slack
>   From my first entrance in,
> Drew nearer to me, sweetly questioning,
>   If I lack'd any thing.
>
> A guest, I answer'd, worthy to be here:
>   Love said, You shall be he.
> I the unkinde, ungratefull? Ah my deare,
>   I cannot look on thee.
> Love took my hand, and smiling did reply,
>   Who made the eyes but I?
>
> Truth Lord, but I have marr'd them: let my shame
>   Go where it doth deserve.
> And know you not, sayes Love, who bore the blame?
>   My deare, then I will serve.
> You must sit down, sayes Love, and taste my meat:
>   So I did sit and eat.
>   *George Herbert*

This poem made a profound impact on me. One reason, I believe, is that I was in stillness. Another reason was that I was being cherished by the Sisters who were incarnating the divine love that the poem describes so poignantly. Yet another reason was that they were praying for me. Consequently the scene was set, not only for God to bid me welcome, but for me to make my response.

When I read the first line, God's magnetic love drew me. One part of me was responding in the depths of my being, sensing, perhaps, that this is what I had been longing for all my life. Another part of me was responding so joyfully that, as I walked to the beach that afternoon and saw and heard the screeching seagulls circling round the bay, *I* wanted to fly with similar abandon. Yet, like the poet, a part of my soul drew back. As I ponder now, with the wisdom of hindsight, what it was that I lacked, I believe that it was permission 'to be' in a sustained way. I was giving myself permission on the retreat and relishing it. What was to happen, though, when I returned home to the Rectory, the parish and the family? After all, deeply ingrained in my spirit were slogans like 'saved to serve', 'Satan finds work for idle hands to do', 'Go into all the world and preach the Gospel to every creature.' Was 'wasting time with God' really acceptable or was it wasting time full stop?

The Book

Ten years after I had begun to explore contemplative prayer, a review copy of *God of Surprises* by Gerard Hughes 'happened' to arrive on my desk. This book seemed as though it had been penned for me at this moment in time.

The author, a Jesuit and skilled spiritual director, had produced a guide book that provides pilgrims with a series of signposts to help them to negotiate life's inner journey. He encourages readers to pause from time to time, to pause and interact with these insights, insisting that, as they do so, they will glean information about *themselves* that will prove to be far more relevant and significant to their lives than anything he had written. He also reminds readers that the inner journey is not linear. The route spirals through many layers of our consciousness. This means that, while we may have encountered the God of surprises at one level of our being, other parts of ourselves, like our feelings for example, may have remained untouched or even closed to God's Spirit.

Page after page of this book prodded me to reflect on and seek to understand the way I had travelled so far. The book challenged me to examine, for example, whether the picture of God I had painted on the walls of my heart was accurate or inaccurate. The book also spread before me a smorgasbord of methods of prayer and of meditating on the Bible – practices that I still use today: seventeen years later! One such method is *lectio divina* – where a passage of Scripture is read as *slowly* as possible resulting in one word or phrase being savoured until its message wings its way into our heart.[3] Another method of praying the Scriptures was *imaginative contemplation* of a gospel narrative where we project ourselves into, say, the room where the disciples were sitting on the first Easter day. We sit with the disciples and, with them, watch the risen one arrive and show us his hands and his side.

My copy of this book is peppered with ticks and comments like: 'Yes', 'Very helpful', 'Superb', 'Lovely', so I was delighted, a few months later, to have the opportunity to make a retreat with the author. At the end of this individually guided retreat, he encouraged me to train in this kind of retreat work. Part of my training was to work alongside him and be supervised by him when he led group retreats. As my own life was enriched and as I watched retreatants' lives being transformed, I longed that my husband, now steeped in parish work, should benefit from the rich fare on which I was feasting. When he attended a similar retreat he found it so meaningful that, when the time arrived for us to leave Nottingham, we went on a 30-day silent retreat together. In the silence, a vision of the chapter of our life we are now living unfolded: we would set up a retreat centre to which missionaries and aid workers could come to have their own spiritual resources replenished. For the past ten years, we have been engaged in this work both in England and in far-flung parts of the world: a hidden ministry inspired by God through reading 'one of the great books of spiritual guidance'.[4]

My Philosophy of Life

In his book *Love Bade Me Welcome*, Robert Llewelyn encourages us to meditate on 'my' poem. He likens George Herbert's feelings of unworthiness to the sentiments expressed by the younger brother in Jesus' parable of the prodigal son. Perhaps *my* predicament when I read it was that I felt more like the elder brother in Jesus' story. This son worked dutifully for his father day in and day out. Their relationship, however, lacked the oneness that comes from a mutuality of understanding that is born and fostered by spending time together. My so-called 'quiet times' up to this point in my life were busy times: in-depth Bible study followed by intercessory prayer. Similarly, my days were so filled with activity *for* God that there was little time simply to be *with* him.

On that retreat, Love took my hand in a way in which the father in Jesus' parable longed, I believe, to take his eldest son's hand when this son stood on the doorstep of the family home hurling insults and abuse at his father.

'Did the elder brother come into the banquet?' asks Professor Kenneth Bailey when commenting on this parable. The only way we discover the answer to that question,' he suggests, is to ask ourselves: 'Will *I* go into the banquet?' By the time this memorable retreat ended, I had not only gone into the banquet, I had sampled spiritual delicacies that ensured that my diet could never be the same again. Love had invited me to sit down and taste his meat – the meat of silence and solitude, the meat of the Eucharist, the meat of savouring as well as studying Scripture.

Through *Love Bade Me Welcome*, Robert Llewelyn nudged me towards a new philosophy of life. One of the chapters of the book is entitled 'Sitting Still in the House'. One section seeks to answer the question: 'How may *we* learn the prayer of stillness?' It seemed as though Robert had written these pages for me. Describing the method of Bible reading that I had been taught, he explained that it often happens that this form of discursive Bible meditation no longer provides a person with the spiritual nurture they most need. The reason, he hastens to add, is that, far from having become less committed to God or less eager to feast on his Word, they are in fact discovering within themselves an insatiable longing for God and for God alone. In the stillness they simply want to be in his presence – not to learn about him but purely to be with him. They are no longer content to learn *about* this Friend. They want to experience his love and friendship and to rest in it.

'Yes, yes, yes' my heart seemed to cry. Over a period of years, this cry gave rise to a resolve to live differently. This is, perhaps, best summed up with a picture: the picture of the human hand. Just as the fingers and the thumb seem to flow from the palm, so in future, I decided, everything that I wrote or did would flow from the Love who bids us welcome. I would carve out time each day to be in that loved place with him so that my relationships and work in the home, the church, the city, my study and my counselling room would all be tinged with the Love that had welcomed me.

Does anyone ever aspire to their own philosophy of life? If they do, maybe I should describe the above, not as a philosophy of life but rather 'my desire' or my goal. As someone has put it: 'We fall and get up, fall and get up, fall and get up again.'

ROBERT LLEWELYN

Robert Llewelyn, born in 1909, is an Anglican priest living in retirement in Norwich. He is the author of *With Pity Not With Blame* (DLT, reprinted 2003), *A Doorway to Silence* (DLT, 1986) and several other books, the latest being *Thirsting for God* (DLT, 2000). He is the editor of *Circles of Silence* (DLT, 1994). He was warden at Bede House, Staplehurst before becoming chaplain at the Julian Shrine in 1976. His earlier ministry was spent in schools or parishes in England, India and Nassau. In 1994 he was awarded the UK individual Templeton Prize and in 1998 the Cross of St Augustine – both in recognition of his contribution to literature in Christian spirituality.

The Person

Of the many people who have influenced me I must give first place to Julian of Norwich. I have increasingly come to understand that nothing is more important for a person of whatever faith than the possession of a right vision of God. The more sincere we are, the more true this must be. Standing alone, sincerity may well do more harm than good. The footballer who has lost his bearings by 180 degrees may be the most sincere person on the field as he kicks a goal for the opposing side. And if we are 180 degrees off true in our vision of God the damage we may do in the conviction that God is well-pleased is incalculable. This is true, not only of violent extremists, but of the many who influence others as broadcasters or journalists, preachers or politicians, men and women in whatever field of communication. If a writer or speaker, ruler or leader, is seriously off target in their vision of God then, in proportion to the sincerity which binds them to their faith, they will be propagating error in the conviction that they are disseminating truth. Hence the dangers to which we are exposed today.

Thomas Merton called Julian a true theologian and by that he meant that he considered her vision of God to be true. It is here that my indebtedness to Julian lies. Julian has enlarged and corrected my inadequate and sometimes mistaken understanding of God. I have yet far to go in absorbing her teaching but she has, I believe, pointed the way.

Mother Julian, as she is often known, was born near the end of

1342 and at the age of 30 experienced, on 8 and 9 May 1373, 16 revelations of the love of God. She probably wrote them down within a few months but 20 years later a greatly expanded version was ready bearing the fruit of her meditations on what she had been shown. Thus we have a longer and shorter version of her shewings. The *Revelations of Divine Love* is translated into many languages (a Russian edition is now on the way) and is recognised as a spiritual classic throughout the Christian world. It is thought to be the first book written by a woman in the English language.

Almost nothing is known of Julian herself. What seems established is that she became an anchoress in a little cell attached to the south wall of St Julian's Church in Norwich and remained there until her death. That date is unknown but is generally assumed to be about 1420. It is unlikely that we even know Julian's baptismal name, the name Julian being probably taken from that of the church which would then have been about 400 years old.

The Book

My second gold ring must, of course, be Julian's book. The *Revelations of Divine Love* is described by a scribe editor as 'a sublime and wonderful revelation of the love of God'. Simply to read the book slowly and meditatively without stopping to consider the difficult passages (that will be a rewarding occupation later) is to expose oneself to be drenched in the love of God. God's inexhaustible love is revealed to Julian as pure compassion. There can be no wrath, she insists, in this all-compassionate God. The wrath is in us and not in God, a wrath waiting to be dissolved in the warmth of God's love. If Julian were writing in today's terms she would be saying that we project our own wrath on to God and see it as God's wrath directed towards ourselves. But Julian is no sentimentalist as will be evident to anyone familiar with her writings.

One of the strange-sounding corollaries springing from this understanding of God is (as Julian states) that theologically speaking, God cannot forgive us our sins. God cannot forgive us because he has at no point been unforgiving. God's compassionate love has been always reaching out towards us, even while we were in our sins, and there is nothing we can do to turn that love into wrath. This thinking is firmly in line with the understanding of the first cry of Jesus from the cross. He had already forgiven his persecutors though there had been no sign of turning on their part. The forgiveness was already there, though it is of course true that it could not be consummated, made active within themselves, until they had turned to him in penitence and faith. Julian insists that the turning must always belong to us and not to God. 'When we pray, the soul is made responsive to God. There is no kind of prayer which can make God more responsive to the soul, for God is always constant in love.' It was Julian who led me to believe in an all-compassionate father who never ceases to draw me to himself. This does not mean that I do not have to suffer as I am cleansed in the purifying fire of God's love. What it means is that in my suffering God is always on my side. And it is this which makes the difference between hope and despair.

Theology and life are inextricably linked and our vision of God must necessarily affect our daily living. Thus if God's compassionate love is always directed towards us it follows that our own love must be so directed towards one another. There can be no saying to my neighbour, 'You say you are sorry, and then I will forgive you.' I must forgive him before he repents even though forgiveness can only be consummated after he has turned again. Though he spurns my offer, it does not belong to me to withdraw it. Indeed it is in the power of my ongoing love towards him that his heart is likely to be softened and so enable us to become friends again. But not only here but at every point, assuming I am sincere in my faith, my thoughts and prejudices will be influenced by my image of God. I have written elsewhere:

> The one who worships a Father Christmas God will be kindly and spoiling and sentimental. The devotees of a policeman God will have their eyes set on law rather than grace. If for some, God is seen mainly as the Almighty judge, then they themselves are likely to be censorious and judgemental. If our God is bigoted and narrow we shall be that way too, intolerant of other faiths and other denominations than our own. The God of Battles will make for a warlike tribe or nation. The early settlers in South Africa were religious people whose conception of a racialist God has left its mark on centuries of history.[1]

And so we might go on. No wonder the universities of old regarded theology as the queen of the sciences! Would that their vision had often been closer to Julian's who bids us look to a God 'who loves us and enjoys us' and wants us to 'love him and enjoy him and firmly trust him, and all shall be well'. 'He is quick to clasp us to himself' she writes, 'for we are his joy and his delight and he is our salvation and our life.'

Space has allowed me to touch only on what has most affected me. The full riches of Julian's book must be left to interested readers to search out on their own.

The Place

The third gold ring must of course be Norwich and especially that acre of it (half a mile south of the Anglican cathedral) which contains St Julian's Church and garden, the Julian Cell, the Julian Centre and All Hallows. It is here that pilgrims come from all over the world, mostly to spend a period of silence on the spot hallowed by Julian's life. I was invited in 1976 to come to Norwich to be chaplain at the cell (my first experience of Julian), a position which I occupied for 14 years though my association with it remains. I was expected to be present in the cell for much of each day, to be attentive to the needs of visitors, and to be responsible for the sale of books and cards, though in a minute way compared with what is offered at the centre today. The cell was also to be a base for the conducting of retreats which happened to be largely in religious houses in which there was an awakening interest in Julian at that time.

The Julian Centre, situated off St Julian's Alley about 50 yards above the church, is a welcoming place, ably and devotedly administered by two assistants who attend to visitors' needs in the selling of books and cards and in directing them, if needed, to books in its well-stocked library. All Hallows next door is staffed by one or more sisters from the Community of All Hallows at Ditchingham 12 miles away. Here visitors are made welcome from near and far. There is often something specially appealing about Julian people and they come from many lands to share their treasure.

The Poem

For my poem, I move to George Herbert and choose *Love bade me welcome* (also known as *Love (III)*). It must be allowed to stand for itself with a brief comment on the unexpected turn it takes in the last two lines.

Love bade me welcome: yet my soul drew back,
　Guiltie of dust and sinne.
But quick-ey'd Love, observing me grow slack
　From my first entrance in,
Drew nearer to me, sweetly questioning,
　If I lack'd any thing.

A guest, I answer'd, worthy to be here:
　Love said, You shall be he.
I the unkinde, ungratefull? Ah my deare,
　I cannot look on thee.
Love took my hand, and smiling did reply,
　Who made the eyes but I?

Truth Lord, but I have marr'd them: let my shame
　Go where it doth deserve.
And know you not, sayes Love, who bore the blame?
　My deare, then I will serve.
You must sit down, sayes Love, and taste my meat:
　So I did sit and eat.

On being accepted by Love our first inclination, as with the guest
in the poem, is to see how we may serve. But no, says Love, you
must allow me to serve you. 'You must sit down', says Love, 'and
taste my meat.' I have needed to learn that being is more
important than doing. That is not because doing is unimportant
but because right doing springs from right being. Before Love
has cleansed us our doing may often disguise rather than express
our being. And so we must allow Love to purge us, a painful
process as our hidden motives are brought to the light which can
dispel the darkness within. It is this which prayer accomplishes
and more especially that which is expressed in the silence of the
heart before God. St John of the Cross expounds this process in
the various dark nights of the soul leading for the elect to the
unitive experience with God. In George Herbert's vision it is the
Mary in us to which we should attend before Martha has her
way.

My Philosophy of Life

For my philosophy of life, I must begin with a story. I picture a village in India which has all it needs to maintain a simple social life, everything that is, except for water. There is a large tank which the rain kept filled in better days and a distance away there is a well whose water can be used only by transferring it bucket by bucket. Every time a villager puts aside some personal preference in order to make instead a return trek across the fields they are pouring into that village the water of life. As the bucket is brought homewards its bearer can have no idea what this pail of water will do. Will it ease the last moments of a dying child, or fertilise a tiny piece of land, or be there for the washing of clothes or the scrubbing of a floor? Who can say? But the water is brought, immersed in the common pool of healing, and that is enough.

We live in a global village and all that we do is interrelated. To each of us is offered the grace to bring the water of life to our stricken world. St Paul bids us to pray without ceasing and this is something to which we may all aspire (however far we may remain from its realisation), seeing prayer as the inclination of the heart towards God rather than the movement of the lips, though it is the second which will be needed to establish the first.[2] Every love-inspired prayer (and love[3] does not have to be felt to be real), vocal or silent, is as a bucket filled with the water of life. We have no idea how God will use that prayer, nor do we ask. It is enough that we put aside our natural sloth and with such love and devotion as is given us offer what we can to be joined with the aspirations of people of goodwill in every place. It is revealed to Julian that we are to pray wholeheartedly even though we find no joy in it, 'for it does good'. At the very least it does good to ourselves and that good cannot help affecting the next person we meet and so a chain reaction is set up. But (as I believe) it goes well beyond that. Somehow, somewhere, in answer to every prayer or praise uttered, prayerful silence observed, or loving deed performed – and this in awareness of our brokenness and need responding to transforming grace as portrayed so movingly in our poem above – good overcomes evil, light dispels darkness, truth supplants error and, if only in the minutest measure, the world is changed.[4]

On 25 April 2002, there died in Buenos Aires at the age of 102 a remarkable lady, Indian by name though European by birth. Indra Devi was still doing her yoga headstand in her late nineties. But more important was her philosophy of life: 'You give love and light to everyone, those who love you, those who harm you, those whom you know, those whom you don't know. It makes no difference. You just give light and love.' 'At eventide' says St John of the Cross, 'they will examine you in love' and he tells us that where there is no love we are to pour love in and we shall draw love out. No matter how far we fall behind the saints of every faith the way is open for our sacrifice to be made in the knowledge that even a cup of water lovingly offered will not be despised.

'Love was his meaning.' In but a few words, Julian of Norwich has said it all.

MICHAEL MARSHALL

Michael Marshall graduated from Christ's College, Cambridge and Cuddesdon Theological College, Oxford. After a period of six years as Vicar of All Saints' Church, Margaret Street, London, he became Suffragan Bishop of Woolwich in 1975 where he remained until 1984. In that year he became the founding Episcopal Director of the Anglican Institute in St Louis, Missouri. During the following eight years he travelled widely across the United States and Canada preaching, lecturing and broadcasting at Mission Centres of the Anglican Institute across North America. As a musician, he has played with the Royal Philharmonic Orchestra, the St Louis Symphony Orchestra and the London Mozart Players. In 1990 he played the Double Mozart Piano Concerto with Raymond Leppard and has given numerous recitals and concerts in the UK, the USA, South America and Africa. In 1992 he returned to the UK as Advisor in Evangelism to the Archbishop of Canterbury and served in this capacity for five years. In 1997 he was appointed as Assistant Bishop of London, based at Holy Trinity, Sloane Street where he continues to serve as Bishop in Residence and was subsequently appointed as Rector in 2002. The Bishop has published many books and writes regularly for *The Church of England Newspaper*.

The Person

I was once told that if and when you had been in the presence of a saint, you would leave with a new sense of confidence in God's love for you, linked together with a determination to try to do better! Well, that was always my experience whenever I have spent time with Eric Abbot, perhaps best known as a former Dean of Westminster.

For many years, Eric served as my spiritual director, or soul friend, as we sometimes term such a ministry. I was but one of many who experienced that precious and much neglected ministry in the church today, at the hands of Eric. There was always more light in the room where Eric was; more fun and godly merriment as with gentle teasing he would help you to say and share things about yourself that you never thought you could ever share with anybody. His speaking voice both informally and formally betrayed a quality and beauty which made you feel that he had been where you had been and knew instinctively the deepest, as well as the darkest of human experiences. (The survival of radio in an age dominated by television reinforces the fact that the human voice is just as distinctive, unique and personal as the features and profile of the human face.)

Then there was what I can only describe as the magic of his loving attention through every moment that you were in his company. As is often said of the great – 'You might have been the only person in the world for the time you were with him.' He greeted you with overwhelming pleasure at your appearance and always accompanied you to the front door to say farewell with an engaging wave of the hand. Then there were the little postcards you would receive on your birthday that carried the reassurance that Eric had remembered you in his prayers that day. You were 'special' except it was not long before you discovered that there were so very many others for whom Eric cared spiritually who also received a cheerful and prayerful postcard on their special days. In large generous handwriting he kept up throughout his life a huge personal correspondence, which was the visible and tangible expression of his life of intercessory prayer.

One among many of his favourite quotations was from George Herbert: 'But above all the heart must bear the longer part.' For Eric had made that longest of all journeys – the journey from head to heart – and had through contemplative prayer, the prayer of the heart, transformed merely intellectual knowledge and information into that higher form of knowledge, best expressed as love. This was perhaps most evident in his style of preaching which warmed the heart and fired the will. In a word, Eric brought out the best in people as a pastor, a preacher and priest. Both the church and the world were colder for me and countless others, the day Eric died.

And his secret? He had discovered what it was and is to be essentially human – warts and all. He refused to be daunted by massive failures in others because one must assume that he was first in touch with his own and had yet also discovered the sufficiency of God's grace as the unqualified remedy for the human tragedy. I can hear him even now saying with a quiet reassuring confidence: 'In the New Testament, Jesus is never shocked by our sins. He is shocked by our fears, but never by our sins.'

The Book

Undoubtedly the book that has had the greatest effect upon my life, after the Bible, is *Confessions* by St Augustine. I go back and back to it again and again.

Of course, like most people, I knew of the book for many years and had made several attempts to read it but gave up after reading the first few pages which in rather poor translations came across to me on first reading as being somewhat tortuous and even unduly introspective. Then several years after my ordination I took the book with me for a week's retreat, determined to stick at it and to finish it in the course of the week.

It was Laurens van der Post who once said: 'If you haven't a story to tell, you haven't a life to live.' Augustine's story is a story worth telling and retelling about a life that eventually was truly and supremely a life worth living. His story unashamedly tells of his struggles and failures; of a journey in which, for much of the time, he was running away from God. For the first 33 years of his life, Augustine shopped around the supermarket of the religious options of his day, of which there were many – not unlike our own day. His personal life all the while was driven by rampant ambition and pride, expressed through reckless and tortuous relationships, culminating in a liaison with an unnamed mistress who gave birth to their illegitimate son.

Then at just that point when Augustine seemed to have achieved success and prominence in his career, his life fell apart in what we would nowadays call a breakdown. Yet it is precisely at that point of break*down* that God breaks *through* and Augustine discovered for himself the truth of which St Paul writes when he tells us that God's strength is made perfect in our weakness. For it is not so much our sins and weaknesses that will rob us of heaven, but rather those strengths and talents which we fail to acknowledge as gifts from an all-sufficient God.

In so many ways I have discovered an uncanny resonance between Augustine's story and my own. It takes a lifetime and more to realise fully that it is the free unearned gift of grace and grace alone that can save us from ourselves – from both our strengths and weaknesses, and furthermore that when we offer our weaknesses to God, he and he alone can transform them into real and authentic strengths. But that realisation does not happen all at once (it certainly did not for Augustine). It is a long and frequently painful process – two steps forward and one step back! That was St Paul's experience and St Augustine's, so I need not be ashamed to own that it is also mine, accompanied however with the joyful realisation that God's grace at every point on the long journey of faith is indeed 'sufficient'. It is not for nothing that Augustine is sometimes referred to as the Doctor of Grace.

The Place

I first stumbled across the Protestant Community of Taizé, in France in the sixties, shortly after I had been ordained. After studying theology, taught as it was then and indeed still is, with an intellectual aridity, I was ready prey for the warmth and love experienced by hundreds of thousands of people who have gone on pilgrimage to Taizé, located not very far from Cluny, the place of monastic renewal in the Middle Ages. There is generally speaking a geography to God's free gift of renewal throughout the ages, both for the wider Church and also personally in our own faith journeys. Yes, of course God is everywhere, but he is strangely and mysteriously more in some places than in others – places of his own choosing, since the wind of the Spirit blows where it wills and nobody can programme or manage the gifts of that Spirit.

As I climbed the hill up to the 'Church of Reconciliation' at Taizé, I was overwhelmed with the huge numbers of young people from many nations who were making their way towards the Community Church which had no architectural merit whatever. But once inside! Just having emerged from the minimalist worship in vogue at that time when we were exhorted to make services 'understandable' (whatever that might mean) I discovered the power of transcendent worship as a converting experience.

What was it about this worship that moved me so profoundly? After all, the services were only adaptations of monastic services, admittedly with beautiful singing, punctuated with long periods of silence. Yet the worship unashamedly borrowed from many different traditions – the icons in the church spoke of the Orthodox churches of the East; the incense and candles more of the Western Catholic traditions; the love of and reverence for Scripture read slowly and prayerfully followed by spontaneous prayer and choruses chanted by the whole congregation was vaguely reminiscent of the reformed churches of Europe. At Taizé all these various traditions converge to enrich the quality of the worship so that it was evident, as T. S. Eliot writes, that Taizé was and is a place where 'prayer is validated'.

Since those days of my first visits, I have frequently revisited Taizé and have been privileged to partake a little in the life of the community. It was there that I discovered the reality of that verse from Genesis – 'It is not good for man to be alone.' For God is essentially 'persons-in-community' and in so far as we are made in God's image we come to the fullness of our humanity when we discover our place in community and in the communion of saints. So it was that Taizé soon came to be for me the place of love as well as worship, the place of prayer and praise and it was not long before I discovered that such places constitute the breeding ground of the true radicals of history, for whom there is no antithesis between the gospel and the so-called social gospel.

In the study groups which take place every day, the community as well as the thousands of visitors engage with the issues confronting our torn and broken world, for clearly when the worship is ended then indeed the service begins. It is, as it has always been, the vision discovered in worship that recalls us to the service of God and our neighbour, as it did for Isaiah of old.

Yes, Taizé is for me, as for so many others, the place of encounter and what I might want to call holistic Christianity. Throughout history disciples have always needed shrines and holy places *somewhere*, so that as God's spies they can go out and discover, recover and uncover that same glory of God *everywhere*.

The Poem

Love (III) by George Herbert

> Love bade me welcome: yet my soul drew back,
>   Guiltie of dust and sinne.
> But quick-ey'd Love, observing me grow slack
>   From my first entrance in,
> Drew nearer to me, sweetly questioning,
>   If I lack'd any thing.

A guest, I answer'd, worthy to be here:
  Love said, You shall be he.
I the unkinde, ungratefull? Ah my deare,
  I cannot look on thee.
Love took my hand, and smiling did reply,
  Who made the eyes but I?

Truth Lord, but I have marr'd them: let my shame
  Go where it doth deserve.
And know you not, sayes Love, who bore the blame?
  My deare, then I will serve.
You must sit down, sayes Love, and taste my meat:
  So I did sit and eat.

It's taken me a lifetime and 40 years of gospel ministry, preaching the good news of God's overriding and unqualified love, to others, yet only latterly have I begun to come perhaps somewhere near the insight of George Herbert as he expresses it in this poem. For many years I was always primarily aware of my unworthiness to receive and to accept the 'loving kindness' of God. I always 'drew back' from the beckoning of the numinous in the presence of God with a sense of guilt and failure, always with the resolution that some day I might achieve some measure of worthiness, little realising what a trap I was in. I felt that I had to search for God and climb some ladder of virtue to come into his presence.

C. S. Lewis says that it is as ridiculous to speak of man looking for God, as it is to speak of a mouse looking for a cat! On the contrary, the cat is looking for the mouse and the mouse had better look out! So, 'herein is love' says St John: 'Not that we loved God, but rather that he first loved us.' True love will always go out of its way, all the way from heaven to earth and hell and back again to meet us at our point of need. That is the nature of God's mission – Emmanuel: God with us in the midst of it all; God with us in the mess of it all; God with us in the mystery of it all.

So it is God's initiative in all of this that has finally overwhelmed me with a Love that has always been there from the beginning, but which a sense of sin and guilt has for too long obscured God's all-embracing love in Christ. So I can now say with the hymn-writer: 'My song is love unknown/My Saviour's love for me.' Or to use

Pauline language, I suppose I am at last beginning to accept with deep gratitude the all-sufficiency of God's grace to cover all my sin. For the last word – the very last word – is gratitude, not guilt and 'thank you' must ultimately overtake even that other fundamental word – 'sorry'.

My Philosophy of Life

'All will be well; all manner of things will be well' sums up the philosophy of life for that remarkable fourteenth-century mystic, Dame Julian of Norwich. At the first take, such an overriding outlook on life in our tragic world might appear to be bland and out of touch with the pain and grief of the human story. St Paul re-affirms this same apparently optimistic philosophy when he says: 'All things work together for good for those who love God.' What, we might well ask, was this optimistic philosophy of life based upon in the real world either of the first century, the fourteenth century or perhaps even more so in the world of our own day?

Certainly I could not embrace such an optimistic philosophy unless I had first embraced the historical facts of the cross and the resurrection as being fundamental to any diagnosis of the human condition. Without those two fundamental historic facts, the human story would appear to be one of unrelenting disaster, while the prognosis – not least at this point in history – would be very dark, inevitably leading to despair.

Yet it is the belief in a God who has brought and continues to bring good out of evil, as was so powerfully and dramatically mani-fested in the cross and resurrection of Jesus, which enables us to replace despair with that deeply Christian virtue of hope, appro-priated by faith and trust in this same God who said 'Let light shine out of darkness'. For this light shines in the darkness and the darkness has not and cannot overwhelm it.

In my own experience, I can readily testify to the powerful reversal that the paradox of the cross and the resurrection has meant in my own life. Many times I have, along with Job, cried out: 'Where on earth is God in all of this?' because in prospect every-thing seems so meaningless and pointless. So often it is only in ret-rospect that we look back and discover that the same paradoxical reversal of the cross and resurrection has been played out in our sto-ries and that we are able to say with a quiet confidence: '*All* things work together for good for those who are anchored in God and in His purposes.' It may be years before we can say that and perhaps for many only after death itself, yet nevertheless such a philosophical manifesto really is the shape of things to come in the loving providence of God.

Almost every day in my evening prayers, I find myself asking the good Lord to 'take the fragments and loose ends of the past day' and to weave them into the tapestry of his loving providence for me, for the church and for his world. At this point of course I am standing on the wrong side of the loom where that tapestry is being woven and much of the time I only see loose ends and no pattern or purpose. Yet, at the end of the day, on my last day I shall by God's grace go to the other side of the loom and see for myself that indeed *all* those apparently meaningless disasters, the good, the bad and the indifferent, have been taken by God and woven into the ultimate reality of his eternal loving purposes and so be able to say along with Dame Julian and all God's saints: 'Yes, all is well, all manner of things are well. Alleluia.' Needless to say, 'It is of course the Lord's doing' from first to last and 'it is indeed marvellous in our eyes'.

ADALBERT MISCHLEWSKI

Adalbert Mischlewski was born in Berlin in 1919. He was engaged as a radio operator in the air force on the French coast during the Second World War. After the war he studied at Munich University reading history, French and English and later Catholic theology. He served as a priest in the Allgäu until 1964, graduating as Doctor of Divinity in 1968. He subsequently taught R.E. and with papal permission, married in 1972. Since retirement in 1983 he has remained active in ecumenical educational work and in 1991 he founded the Antoniter-Forum, a scientific-cultural society with members in various European countries. He continues to serve as their Chairman and Editor of the Yearbook and is much in demand for presentation of papers at conferences in Germany and abroad.

The Person

My first fifty years were spent almost entirely among persons of my own sex – twelve years in boys' schools with no female teachers, seven years labour and military service to 1945, a period from 1946 to 1950 studying history and modern languages, in those years establishing and organising Catholic male students' groups ('Neudeutschland'), then three years in a seminary training for the priesthood and finally service as a Catholic priest from 1954.

As a priest I led evening services and spiritual talks for students and teachers in a boarding school. It was there that, already fifty years old, I came to know the person who has had the most profound and lasting effect on my life. In 1970 I met and grew to know and love Johanna, a teacher at the school. And I then had to face the hard decision whether to remain a priest, a role I really loved, or to choose a life with her – a decision finally taken during a retreat after an intense talk with its spiritual leader.

That decision was to change my life completely. Until then I had mostly been in situations where I had to try to win recognition in a defensive way – as a Catholic among Protestants, as a Christian among non-believers, as an intellectual among materialists, as a city-dweller in the country, as a reform-conscious person among traditionalists. Now the time had come to learn something new – sharing others' concerns, observing and understanding them, regarding them in a generous and sympathetic way. This difficult learning process was only possible through the almost inexhaustible patience of my wife. That I myself have gained a little more patience – still not enough! – I owe to her. I have learned not to give up too soon, to try every available course and to exhaust all possibilities.

It was of decisive consequence that Johanna came from a deeply faithful Lutheran family. Although greatly interested in ecumenical affairs and for years a member of an ecumenical study group, I found a completely new world opening to me through sharing services, discussion and simple everyday experiences.

New impulses for my spiritual life, however, counted most for my further life. From the beginning of our relationship we practised shared prayer. What was new to me and what I learned was personal prayer in a comprehensive sense until then unknown to me. As a Catholic priest I had been accustomed to the set prayers of the Eucharist and the Hours, on bringing them to life and explaining them to others.

Although gratefully recognising God's clear guidance in my life and particularly in dangerous situations during the war, I only learned through my wife to perceive God's love even in the most ordinary matters of everyday life, and trustingly to pray and seek it – 'Ask, and it shall be given you' (Matt. 7:7).

So today after 30 years of a happy married life I am still filled with joy and gratitude for God's gift helping me on essentially through this special person who came into my life relatively late.

The Book

Before I realised it was a specific book it had begun its influence. Very early in my life my father took me to morning service on Sundays – my mother went to an early morning Mass, as did all women who had to prepare meals. The Sunday High Mass was dominated by organ music and hymns. Most fascinating for a boy, however, was the reading of the gospel in German before the sermon. The dignified language of the gospel made a deep impression on me, although my mother and my grandmother had told me a great deal about Jesus and had probably read to me from the Children's Bible. Very early my wish was to have a 'Schott' which included the texts of the Latin Mass in German. I received my first New Testament only as a teenager at grammar school.

Ludwig Esch, a well-known Jesuit in the thirties, was the man who kindled my enthusiasm for the texts of the gospels in a spiritual retreat. More than all other books of the Bible I loved the synoptic gospels because in them I could listen to the *ipsissima vox* of Jesus, mainly in his parables, follow his footsteps in the Holy Land and vividly imagine his life. Reading them was and is never repetitive – it deepens knowledge and opens new dimensions. Good commentaries and spiritual sermons are a welcome supplement. The very words of Jesus as they are handed down to us in the first three gospels have gradually become a pointer and yardstick in life which are not always heeded but certainly guide and encourage us. And I know they will guide me through the rest of my life.

The Place

Determined by the war and the circumstances which followed, and later by my profession, I have lived in many different places. But the one which has had the most profound impact is a town whose name did not mean anything to me until after the war.

During my war service on the Channel coast in 1941 I came to know a fellow soldier who was to become a life-long friend because of his genuine Christian faith, a fairly rare stance in the armed forces. His home was in Memmingen, a town of medium size in Bavaria. When we – what an act of providence! – met in February 1945 quite unexpectedly in a Sunday service on the Grafenwöhr (Northern Bavaria) training area he invited me to come to his home and wait there to find how things would develop after the collapse. It was not advisable to go back to my home town of Berlin because of the unpredictable Soviet occupying power.

This was the reason why only three weeks after the capitulation, released as one of the first American prisoners of war, I came to my friend's family in Memmingen and was received like a son. My time there seemed like a new birth in many respects. At last the hated Nazi regime and the merciless war were over and one could talk freely again. Compared with that the many other restrictions, especially those regarding our 'daily bread', carried less weight. Immediately we started building up a Catholic youth organisation in which I was strongly committed. To earn some money I worked as a gardener, a previously unknown sphere for me. The fact that I could live unhindered as a Catholic and was not a member of a small minority, at best smiled at but mostly attacked and mocked, made me feel especially at ease.

In the last months of 1945 the universities began to prepare for reopening, but that in my home town, Berlin, being in Communist hands, did not accept me, a former war officer, whereas the University of Munich took me after some weeks of service removing mountains of rubble from bombed sites. During weekends, however, and semester breaks I lived in Memmingen where an ever-increasing circle of friends, like-minded people and acquaintances helped me to feel at home and where I eventually dropped on my 'life-theme' without having the faintest idea what the consequences would be for me.

Memmingen had been for more than three centuries (1214–1562) the site of an important house of the Antonines, of whom I had never before heard. As at that time hardly any literature existed about this French hospital order, which once spread throughout Europe, and Memmingen housed a large archive, I began to delve into its history. This subject has remained fascinating to this day because it also covers the history of medicine, of mentality and of everyday life. Discovering an order of French origin in a Suebian town has also opened up many friendships with French people.

My involvement with Memmingen grew even closer after I had the opportunity to rescue the fifteenth-century Antonine hospital – unique in Europe – when in the 1980s it was threatened with destruction by a speculator for sheer profit. It is now fully repaired and restored, and used as a public library and museum, displaying its rich history of ministry and healing.

The Poem

Even before reading it myself, I had heard parts of Friedrich von Schiller's *Das Lied von der Glocke* (The Song of the Bell) recited from my mother's lips. In her generation it was quite common to learn the complete poem of over a thousand lines by heart. From hearing it and from the numerous lines that have become familiar quotations I was well acquainted with the ballad before reading it myself for the first time. Our German teacher at grammar school knew how to awaken us to its beauty and depth. Although very rarely getting down to rereading this poem over the years, it has always seemed to me an outstanding peak of poetry.

The poet managed to interweave his description of bell-founding with that of human life in all its joys and sorrows. References to contemporary society are an essential ingredient, too. Schiller, who attached such great importance to freedom, sharply criticises the excesses of the French Revolution and ends the poem with a vision of peace – 'Friede sei ihr erst Geläute!' (Peace be its first chime).

The reason I choose it is for its wealth of ideas and concepts, which never lose their significance. It has moulded my view of a civil society where freedom and peace are predominant.

My Philosophy of Life

First, God as a loving father rather than judge, Jesus Christ really our brother and the Holy Spirit alive in us (Rom. 8:26) – this I learned through one of my most influential mentors in the Catholic Students' Movement.

Secondly, I recognise through numerous experiences, and believe to be invaluable in evaluating situations in one's own life, God's constant guidance in both small and important matters. Consequently one of my principles is neither to claim nor refuse anything. My favourite text is the last line of the Te Deum – 'In te, Domine, speravi, non confundar in aeternum'.

Thirdly, through experiencing examples of extreme unfairness during the pre-war (Reichsarbeitsdienst) and war periods, I have developed a strong sense of justice and believe it is a responsibility of everyone to give his utmost to achieve it. Here I feel supported by the overwhelming cry for justice throughout the Old Testament.

Fourthly, I have become increasingly aware of the importance of the *kairos* – of the fact that the opportunity to effect something, to do something good to others, will not come a second time and has to be seized.

And finally, from this I become more and more impressed by the preciousness of this unique life we have on earth. Each moment, each minute is a valuable gift, in which we are builders of the everlasting life, if we allow God's Spirit to lead us.

MICHAEL PERRY

Canon Michael Perry read chemistry and theology for his degrees at Cambridge in the 1950s and was ordained in 1958. Bishop Ian Ramsey appointed him Archdeacon of Durham and Canon Residentiary of Durham Cathedral in 1970 and he has lived in Durham ever since – now in retirement. He joined the Churches' Fellowship for Psychical and Spiritual Studies in 1978 when he was asked to edit its theological quarterly *The Christian Parapsychologist*; the Fellowship made him its Chairman in 1986 and its President (a position he still holds) in 1998. He has written a number of books on subjects as diverse as the new Holy Communion services, parish finance and psychical research. His most recent is entitled *Psychical and Spiritual* (CFPSS, 2003) and celebrates the Golden Jubilee of the CFPSS.

The Person

Who has had the most profound effect on my life? No doubt about that. Who but the person who has shared every intimate moment with me for the last 40 years? Without Margaret, I cannot begin to imagine what I would be like or where I would now be. My life and hers have been intertwined so closely that it would be neither possible nor profitable to try to disentangle them.

But Margaret aside, who has most helped my life take the direction it has done? I could think of many possibilities – 'Boris' who encouraged my enthusiasm for all things chemical; Stephen, to whom I first confided my belief that I might be called to ordination; Roger, who nurtured me and helped me grow in the faith; Merlin, who trained me as a deacon and remained a lifelong friend.

Perhaps the most influential of them, however, would be Bishop Ian Ramsey. Late one night in the Sheffield diocesan retreat house, after a meeting of the Archbishops' Doctrine Commission to which he had asked me to be secretary, he talked me into a job he wanted me to do in his diocese of Durham. I knew so little about the workings of the church that it never dawned on me till I asked him, what the title was for the post he was asking me to fill. That started me out on a marvellously fulfilling stint of work as a Canon of Durham Cathedral – for the first twenty-three years as Archdeacon and the last five as Bishop's Senior Chaplain.

I was only able to serve Ian personally for a thousand days before the fatal heart attack which took him from us in 1972 but by then I had realised what an extraordinary man he was. He was one of the country's leading philosophers of religion, able to engage academically with the cleverest in the land. He was a man absolutely popping with ideas, who started so many new initiatives in the diocese that it took years after his death to integrate them into the structure of its work. Yet he was also an accessible human being, bubbling with unrepressed friendliness, who so moved the coal-miners of County Durham that they invited him to speak on the same platform as the politicians and union leaders at the great Miners' Gala. It was the first and only time in the long history of that event that a bishop had been asked to do so. I have never been privileged to work with so great a man before or since.

But not even Ian Ramsey could qualify as being the person who has had the most profound effect on my life. There is someone else, whom I have been getting to know better and better as the years have gone by, but whose full significance is still way beyond me. I hope and pray I shall come to a fuller knowledge of him after this life is over. That person is Jesus of Nazareth.

The Book

Which book has had the most profound effect on my life? The Bible, of course. But, that apart, there is one which I read in my formative years which set a significant part of my course for the rest of my time.

When I was a teenager in the late 1940s and early 1950s, I was an avid reader of blue-backed Penguin books on scientific subjects and had the catalogue of new titles regularly posted to me. Every member of the science sixth form had, during his time, to talk to the school Scientific Society on some topic of his own choosing. When my turn came up, I had just read a most unusual book called *The Personality of Man* by G. N. M. Tyrrell. It was about the scientific study of things I had never come across before – faculties of the human mind like telepathy, clairvoyance, automatic writing and psychic sensitivity. As a cradle Christian, there were many teachings I had had to accept on trust – human survival of death was one of them. And now, in this remarkable book, here was a man who told me that it was possible to carry out scientific research which might one day shift this whole subject from the realm of faith to the realm of knowledge.

In more than fifty years since then, I have realised that things are not that simple and my naïve early hopes have had to become a deal more sophisticated. But Tyrrell's book opened a whole realm to me. At first it was solely an intellectual adventure and I joined the Society for Psychical Research to see what academic credentials there were in this particular line of study. But as I grew into the Christian ministry, I began to come across people who needed help in coming to terms with psychic matters. Some of them had been troubled by unwanted psychic disturbances but there were others who seemed to possess some degree of psychic sensitivity and wanted to integrate it within mainstream Christian thought and practice. So I joined the Churches' Fellowship for Psychical and Spiritual Studies and have edited its theological journal *The Christian Parapsychologist* for a quarter of a century. Eventually, the Fellowship has done me the honour of electing me as its President. Is that sufficient for a book to qualify as having been the most influential in my life?

The Place

I have absolutely no doubt which place has had the profoundest effect on me. Every morning until my retirement five years ago, my first action on getting out of bed was to open the shutters and gaze out at the great bulk of Durham Cathedral standing on the far side of College Green from our house.

Sir Walter Scott wrote of its 'grey towers' but he must have seen it on a dull day because the different colours it can take are a continual amazement. Particularly when there is a red sky at night, the rosy glow of the stonework is the eye's delight. And inside! The sheer material solidity of those great stone pillars seems paradoxically to lift the soul to spiritual peaks.

But it is what goes on in that building which engenders the greater wonder. It is not only the great services – the ordinations, the Advent processions and Christmas carol services, the Miners' Gala celebration, the judges of the northern circuits processing in like something from Gilbert and Sullivan. It is not only the musical occasions, though there can be few more splendid places in which to hear Bach's Mass in B Minor or Beethoven's *Missa Solemnis* (or even, on two remarkable occasions, a Eucharist with music from Duke Ellington performed by a jazz band and tap dancer). The daily and weekly round feed the soul at least as much; evensong with sometimes more in the choir than the congregation, morning prayer with a handful of Canons and occasionally a visitor or two, a quiet early morning Eucharist. And, when it looks as if nothing is happening in the building, there is the opportunity to sit and think – or else just sit – whilst the busy world is hushed for long enough for those who have sought spiritual refreshment there to find what it was they were looking for. Amazing things can happen when folk think nothing is happening!

Yes, Durham Cathedral is a place of marvel. Despite having lived in its shadow for so long, I never got to the stage where it was possible to take that building for granted. For me it was, like God's love, new every morning.

The Poem
Neither poetry nor the visual arts have meant a great deal to me, though there are some poems which always have the power to move me. George Herbert's *Love bade me welcome*, for instance, or several by John Donne – the ringing certainties of *Death, be not proud* or *At the round earth's imagined corners, blow your trumpets, angels, and arise, arise from death, you vast infinities of souls*, or the wistful *Wilt thou forgive that sin where I begun?*

For me, it is music rather than poetry which speaks more directly soul to soul. According to mood, I love to bask in the genial faith of Joseph Haydn or the joyful melodies of Wolfgang Mozart. But when I want to contemplate the mysteries of human existence, or think about profundities which I know I will never plumb – or not on this earth, at any rate – it is to Ludwig van Beethoven that I have to go. It is not only that I can empathise with someone who had to work hard to achieve perfection and draft and redraft before he had anything with which he could be satisfied. It is that he can assure me that there are aspects of our existence here which are simply not amenable to intellectual analysis. Like Job, we simply have to kneel before them and wonder.

So I listen again and again, especially to his last quartets, and know I shall never be able to encapsulate in words what they mean but that I can catch some glimpse of a reality which is greater even than the music which hints at it. That reality has gone through great suffering and when it has come out on the other side, the glib assertions of the early works have become transformed into the quiet assurance of the opening of the fourteenth quartet or the deep joy of the alternative final movement of the thirteenth – the last complete movement Beethoven ever wrote, as he was dying in agony. That, for me, is the deepest poetry and greater than any words can evoke.

My Philosophy of Life

When I was about ten years old, I wanted to get to the grammar school and learn about chemistry. It was because my cousin (who was five years older than I was) had told me that if I did so I would be taught how to make gunpowder.

As I grew older, my fascination with chemistry matured and I saw it as a way of finding out how the world was made and what made it work. But that sense of understanding hasn't lasted, as the old simplicities of the 'billiard ball' picture of atomic structure has given way to the mind-bending incomprehensibilities of quantum mechanics. Now, we look into the atom and have a vertiginous sense of its vast emptiness – a simmering sea of fleeting energy-patterns bubbling out of a restless background of zero-point energy – increasingly impossible to understand.

Then I took a second degree, this time in theology. And, again, the original simplicities have needed to be modified as time went on. So many of the things that I once thought to be important now seem to be secondary. For instance, I despair of the people who seem to think that the most significant members of the church are the clergy and that unless they are male and heterosexually inclined, God is unable to use them to turn bread and wine into his body and blood; or Christians who believe that all new starts can be blessed, except the new start after a disastrous marriage with an unsuitable partner.

What for me is primary is an increasing realisation of the living mystery who is God and his love which is shown, especially in Jesus, towards the human race and towards me as a member of it. There is nothing cut-and-dried about *that* mystery. I see through a glass, darkly (and that word 'darkly' is a wonderfully evocative translation of St Paul's original Greek). I do not ever think that I shall know as

I am known – not even in the life of the world to come – because I am a finite creature and God and his ways are infinite. I may never *understand* but I shall, I believe, be *satisfied*.

Does this leave me with a coherent 'philosophy of life'? That is for others to judge. I have had a busy life so far and my philosophy has been always to give of my best, to the glory of God and the good of those who have asked things of me. I may not always have succeeded but I have (as my wife readily acknowledges) always been trying.

So, let my last thinks be thanks – a philosophy of gratitude for everything that life brings. Thanks to the person, the book, the place, and the music which has had the most profound effect on my life but especially thanks to God. He has set me in very pleasant places and given me work to do which has been a joy to undertake. Better than any number of gold rings!

JOHN POLKINGHORNE

For 25 years, John Polkinghorne was a theoretical physicist, working on theories of elementary particles. From 1968 to 1979 he was Professor of Mathematical Physics at Cambridge and was elected an FRS in 1974. He then resigned his chair and studied for the ministry of the Church of England at Westcott House, being ordained priest in 1982. After a few years in parochial ministry, John returned to Cambridge to be Dean of Chapel at Trinity Hall from 1986-89. He then became the President of Queens' College, Cambridge, a position from which he retired in 1996. In 1997 he was made a KBE. In addition to two technical monographs on particle theory, John has written five books on science for the general reader and fifteen books on aspects of the relationship between science and religion. John has been a member of the BMA Medical Ethics Committee, the General Synod of the Church of England, the Doctrine Commission and the Human Genetics Commission. In 2002 he was awarded the Templeton Prize. He is a Fellow of Queens' College, Cambridge and Canon Theologian of Liverpool.

The Person

Of course, the person who has most influenced my life has been my wife, Ruth. We have been married for more than 48 years and there has been much in our life together for which I am profoundly grateful. Ruth is a devout woman and she has always supported me in my own spiritual pilgrimage, including my mid-life adventure of leaving physics to become a priest, a move that had to be a joint decision for us.

My marriage to Ruth has been the private centre of my life but I would like also to pay grateful tribute to someone who has had an important, if somewhat hidden, influence on the more public side of my activity. His name is Eric Hutchison, a Canadian priest and Jungian psychotherapist, long resident in England after a spell teaching theology in Uganda. Eric, his wife Elspeth and their family came to live near us and they worshipped at the same Cambridge church that we did. Eric started a Bible study group in our area to which Ruth went regularly. After about a year, she said to me that I ought to go too, for Eric was an outstanding teacher of Christian truth from whom she was gaining much insight. I was somewhat reluctant to agree – I had a pretty busy life as a professor – but in the end I went along. It was to prove a truly formative influence on me. The group came from diverse backgrounds but Eric was very skilful in facilitating a discussion to which all could contribute. He himself expounded Christian understanding in a way that was stimulating and exciting, faithful to Scripture's power but creatively open to contemporary interpretation. I attended the group for several years, only leaving it when we moved out of the area.

I learned many significant things from Eric but one of the most important was his way of exploring the Bible that was open to its spiritual power in a way that expanded rather than narrowed one's thinking. From our friendship and from many conversations together, I also learned much about myself, as Eric shared some of his deep psychological insights with me.

These experiences helped me to see how theological thinking exceeds even scientific thinking in its insightful power to yield understanding of reality. From seeing something of Eric's priestly ministry (including hearing his powerful preaching) I glimpsed the worthwhile character of that vocation. All this certainly played a significant part in motivating my eventual decision to seek ordination. Eric was an encouraging and sustaining influence during the inevitable ups and downs that accompanied such a transition. When I was ordained priest in 1982, I was grateful that he was able to be the preacher at my ordination.

The Book

After I had been accepted for ordination, there was a period of about 18 months during which I wound up my academic affairs before finally resigning my professorship and going to theological college. After all, I could not just leave my research students with the hope that they might one day get their PhDs. During this time a friend of mine, Keith Sutton, who was the then Principal of Ridley Hall, said to me that I ought to read some serious theology before beginning my formal training. He suggested I started with Jürgen Moltmann's *The Crucified God* (SCM Press, 1974 and 2001). I duly set to work to read it.

Doing so was another great formative influence on me. I was bowled over by the creative power of theological thinking that the book displayed. I suppose that the greatest problem that theology faces is that presented to it by the evil and suffering that we see so widely at work in a world that is claimed to be the creation of a benevolent and powerful God. I believe that this difficulty holds more people back from religious belief than any other and it is one that continues to trouble those of us who are religious believers. Moltmann takes with absolute seriousness the incarnation – the Word of God made flesh in the human life of Jesus Christ – and with absolute seriousness the darkness and desolation of the cruci-fixion, from which comes the cry, so scrupulously recorded by Matthew and Mark, 'My God, my God, why have you forsaken me?' Moltmann sees this profound gospel incident as Jesus becoming 'the kind of man we do not want to be: an outcast, accursed, crucified' so that 'when the crucified Jesus is called "the image of God", the meaning is that this is God, and God is like this'. In other words, the Christian God is not simply a compassionate spectator, looking down in pity on the sufferings of this often bitter world, but he has been a fellow-sufferer in the travail of creation, for the Christian God is the crucified God.

I do not claim that this insight removes all the perplexity and anguish that we feel in the face of suffering but it does meet it at the very deep level that the problem demands. For me, this insight makes belief in God possible, the strangeness of the world notwith-standing. *The Crucified God* is not easy reading, for the seriousness of its theme necessarily makes demands upon the reader and it is a text to whose rereading I have several times returned after that initial encounter. I have also read all of Moltmann's other major books, for he is the contemporary theologian whom I find to be most illumi-nating and helpful. Subsequently I have come to know him a little personally and I have been grateful for our meetings, often taking place in connection with some theological project in which we have both been participants. I am the kind of academically inclined per-son for whom this example of how one can hold the faith with total intellectual integrity is most helpful and significant.

The Place
I have spent far and away the greater part of my life in Cambridge. Not only did I come up in 1949 as an undergraduate at Trinity College reading mathematics, subsequently staying on for a 25-year

career in theoretical physics, and returning again after a few years spent in parish life following my ordination but I even went to school in Cambridge, at the Perse, for the last three years of my secondary education. Ruth and I now live there in retirement.

Cambridge is a city of great beauty, with its many ancient College buildings. My last job was as President of Queens' College, so we lived in the President's Lodge, a late medieval and Tudor building with a handsome long gallery and a panelled dining room, where Cardinal Wolsey and Catherine of Aragon had both stayed in the days when it had been the principal guest apartment. It was an enormous privilege to have such a splendid house as one's home, even if necessarily on a temporary basis.

As an undergraduate I had wandered the courts of Trinity and worshipped in its chapel, given it by Queen Mary. In the antechapel there was Roubilliac's famous statue of Isaac Newton, 'a marble mind forever voyaging through strange seas of thought alone', as Wordsworth said. All the time in Cambridge one is conscious of past history and particularly the history of the intellectual giants of former times. The first Cavendish Professor of Physics was James Clerk Maxwell, a very great scientist indeed and the founder of electromagnetic theory. He had the words of Psalm 111, 'The works of the Lord are great, sought out of all them that have pleasure therein' set in Latin over the entrance archway to his new laboratory. When the Cavendish moved out to more spacious buildings in West Cambridge, the Cavendish Professor of the time, Nevill Mott, had the same words (but now in English) set over the new entrance.

Cambridge is certainly a heritage city but it is not at all in thrall to the past, being perpetually intellectually lively in its continuing life. I remember that a party of Russian scientists who were visiting Trinity were shocked to find that Newton's old rooms were not preserved as a museum but were occupied by a contemporary academic. But that is exactly the point, for the Colleges are living institutions, inspired by the past to continue the pursuit of knowledge in the present.

No place is perfect, however. As a West Country man, used in childhood to the hills and moors, I must confess to finding the fens that surround Cambridge as being somewhat boring – great skies of course but not a great deal else it seems to me. Erasmus (who was the most important person ever to be associated with Queens') complained after his time in Cambridge that the east wind was cold (true) and the beer was thin (no longer true). Nevertheless, it has been a great privilege to have spent so much of my life in this East Anglian city of plain living and high thinking.

The Poem

I have an embarrassing confession to make. I am a very prosaic sort of person. I love writing – the means by which I crystallise out my thought from the cloud of ideas swirling around in my head – and I read a great deal of prose, but poetry is rather a blind spot for me. I do not read very much of it and I have not tried to write a poem myself since not very successful attempts at enforced versification were required of me at school.

If I have to choose a poet, I shall go for George Herbert. He was a Fellow of Trinity College, Cambridge and subsequently a country parson and in these respects, at least, we have things in common. Herbert seems to me to be the perfect example of devout but moderate Anglican piety. My favourite among his poems is the well-known *Love bade me welcome* with its moving portrayal of Christ graciously greeting the hesitant sinner.

Having said all that, there is in fact a form of poetry that I read every day. As an Anglican priest, I have a duty to say the morning and evening office, which is an important part of my spiritual discipline. Part of the office focuses on the prayerful recitation of the psalms and a priest works through the whole psalter 'in course' (that is, in order) every ten weeks. I love the psalms, especially because of their spiritual frankness. You find a much wider range of spiritual experience and emotions recorded in the psalter than you will ever find between the covers of a hymn book. In Psalm 44, the writer even tells God to wake up and pay attention to what is happening in the world: 'Rouse yourself, O Lord, why do you sleep? Awake, do not cast us off for ever.' There is a robustness in Jewish spirituality which does not hesitate to argue with God or to complain that I find very attractive and realistic. But it is not all protest. Particularly helpful are the so-called psalms of lament that start with complaint but end with an affirmation of trust in God's steadfast faithfulness, a confidence that surely owes much to the honesty of protest that has preceded it. A perfect example is the short Psalm 13, which I would like to quote in full:

How long O Lord will you so utterly forget me:
how long will you hide your face from me?
How long must I suffer anguish in my soul
and suffer grief in my heart day and night:
How long shall my enemy triumph over me?
Look upon me O Lord my God and answer me:
lighten my eyes lest I sleep in death;
Lest my enemy say 'I have prevailed against him':
lest my foes exult in my overthrow.
Yet I put my trust in your unfailing love:
O let my heart rejoice in your salvation.
And I will make my song to the Lord:
because he deals so bountifully with me.

My Philosophy of Life

The centre of my life, and the ground on which I seek to base my approach to living, is my Christian faith. I grew up in a Christian home and I cannot recall a time when I was not a member of the worshipping and believing community of the church. Of course, as I grew older my understanding and, I hope, my commitment deepened but I have never faced a crisis of faith, let alone stood outside the Christian community. That has been the particular form of my spiritual pilgrimage. I spend quite a lot of time writing about Christian belief and trying to explain why I hold it, including indicating how I feel able to take both science and religion with great seriousness, regarding them as complementary insights into the rich reality in which we live. I certainly do not want a compartmentalised life – a priest on Sundays and a physicist on Mondays. I am a rather passionate believer in the unity of knowledge.

Central to my Christian faith is the figure of Christ, as I meet him in Scripture, in the church and in the sacraments. No philosophy of life could be satisfactory for me that did not take Jesus fully into account. He is a compelling figure, even if in some ways a mysterious figure. What he has to say is by no means always easy. I feel sympathy with Peter who, after Jesus had said some particularly difficult things that made some of his followers turn away, was asked by Christ, 'Do you also wish to go away?' In an affirmation of trust with a hint of desperation in it, Peter replied, 'Lord, to whom can we go? You have the words of eternal life.' (John 6:66-8). That is what I feel too – I know I have to seek to be on Jesus' side in life.

The strangest thing about Jesus is the way his life appears to end: painfully and shamefully executed, deserted by his followers with a cry of dereliction on his lips. Compared with the peaceful and honoured old age enjoyed by other great religious leaders such as Moses, the Buddha and Mohammed, it all seems a tale of failure. If the story of Jesus had really ended there, I believe that we would be unlikely ever to have heard of him. I believe that the story did not end there but that it continued into an everlasting glorified life after his resurrection on the third day, which vindicated Jesus and gave us all the hope of a destiny beyond our deaths. The characteristic way in which the church has always spoken of Christ is not as a revered founder-figure of the past but as a living Lord in the present.

If the fundamental Christian assertion really is 'Jesus lives!' then Christians must have some experience of this in their own time. For me, this centres on the eucharistic worship of the church, at which I sometimes have the privilege of presiding at the altar on behalf of the gathered community of the faithful. It is not easy to express this adequately but here I find the focus of my spiritual life and the place of meeting with the One I seek to acknowledge as the Lord of my life.

EDWIN ROBERTSON

Edwin Robertson was born in 1912 and is a Baptist minister serving several churches, mostly in London. He has been involved in broadcasting, both as Assistant Head of Religious Broadcasting at the BBC and Executive Director of the World Association for Christian Broadcasting. He was a Senior Control Officer in the British occupation of Germany and has written extensively on Dietrich Bonhoeffer. He has travelled widely as Study Secretary for the United Bible Societies and as a communications consultant.

The Person

The person who has most inspired me was a German Lutheran pastor whom I never met. To be inspired by a person is to have something of his personality – his spirit – take possession of you, influencing the way you live, the way you think and something more which is akin to love. It is not often a sudden flash but a long-drawn-out process. For me, the person was Dietrich Bonhoeffer and the inspiration has grown over 50 years and continues.

A few weeks after the end of the Second World War, I heard of a service to be held at Holy Trinity Church, London to commemorate a German. There, I heard of a German pastor who persistently risked his life and sacrificed his career, as well as his reputation, to oppose the monstrous tyranny which was poisoning his country. I learned that when his friends had taken him to safety in America, he refused to stay because he wanted to be with his people in wartime. It was virtual suicide but he knew what he had to do and did it. The Bishop of Chichester told us of how in the midst of war he had met him in neutral Sweden, trying to persuade the British government to support the resistance movement in Germany.

A little later, I was making contact with German prisoners of war, visiting their camps and worshipping with them, sometimes in my own church when they were allowed out. From their pastor (Schliebitz from Silesia) I learned more of Bonhoeffer and he gave me a booklet being circulated by the Red Cross. It was called *The Witness of an Ambassador* – 58 pages about Bonhoeffer, including some of the poems he wrote in prison. Reading those poems joined my spirit to his. There was courage in them, admission of guilt, a longing for a repentant church, a devotion to his God which made me realise my inadequacy as a minister. From that moment I knew this man was with me for life. It was a path into a new world. In 1947 I went to Germany to the Religious Affairs Branch of the British Control Commission. There, in my official capacity as a Senior Control Officer, I met Bonhoeffer's friends and family – most important of all his twin sister Sabine, who had been deeply attached to him. Her room was full of pictures and models which she had sculpted of his head. Over the years, we have met and talked and until her death a few years ago she was an ever-renewing source of my spiritual contact with her twin brother.

I have written many books about him, translated his poems, his sermons, his letters and much beside. He has never left me, nor do I think he will until death. His integrity in dealing with people, his honesty with himself, his courage and his determination to search out the truth as it is today continues to inspire me. He loved his church but despaired of it. He did what he knew to be right, despite the obvious consequences – including that in doing what was right to him might turn out to be wrong. Rather than argue about whether to do this or that, he did what he believed to be right, prepared to 'sacrifice his righteousness' if need be. I was most inspired by this honest man of deep devotion from whom I cannot escape.

The Book

The book which has had the most profound effect upon my life as a whole has to be the Bible but that is more than a book. I need to search among the thousands of books in my library to see which by its own impact has affected me most. Again and again I come back to a book which I had compiled from another man's writings: *The Price of Success* – the autobiography of J. B. Phillips. We had been colleagues in many ways – broadcasting, translating, enabling churches to improve their means of communication. When he was dying, he said that he was worried that he had signed a contract with the publisher for his autobiography but had not finished it. Rashly, I said I would do what I could. He was deeply relieved. I found myself reading the unfinished manuscript and realising that I had taken on a very difficult task. His widow helped me and over many visits to Swanage, we read all his writings, including his love-letters to her.

We compiled the book as a mosaic of his writings – published and unpublished – until we had J. B.'s story in his own words. The most moving part of it was that of his many years of clinical depression which left him unable to lecture, preach or publish. But what he did do was deal with a vast number of pastoral problems by post with many who had read his books – throughout this country and in the USA. Today there are 15 box files full of this material. The way he handled depression was more wonderful than his superb translation of *Letters to Young Churches*. After so much success, he could describe what happened to him in words that had the most profound effect upon me:

> I was in a state of some excitement throughout the whole of 1955. My work hardly seemed arduous for it was intrinsically exciting. I was tasting the sweets of success to an almost unimaginable degree, my health was excellent, my future prospects were rosier than my wildest dreams could ever suggest, applause, honour, appreciation met me wherever I went ... I was not aware of the dangers of success. The subtle corrosion of character, the unconscious changing of values and the secret monstrous growth of a vastly inflated idea of myself, seeped slowly into me. Vaguely I was aware of this and like some frightful parody of St Augustine, I prayed: 'Lord make me humble – but not yet.'

That passage profoundly influenced me, coming at a time when I could recognise it as relevant to my own life. It has prevented me from ever taking congratulations too seriously. Success and failure are much alike. But there was another passage from his earlier life as a young Anglican priest who was suffering from a serious illness and was not expected to recover. He heard the consultant say, 'He probably won't last the night.' That night he dreamed and described his dream later. Whenever I read that passage with Vera, his widow, she always cried. Here is the dream:

> I was alone, depressed and miserable, trudging wearily down a dusty slope. Around me were the wrecks and refuse of human living. There were ruined houses, pools of stagnant water, cast-off shoes, rusty tin cans, worn out motor tyres and rubbish of every kind. Suddenly, as I picked my way amid this dreary mess,

I looked up. Not far away on the other side of a little valley, was a vista of indescribable beauty. It seemed as though all the loveliness of mountain and stream, of field and forest, of cloud and sky were displayed with such intensity of beauty that I gasped for breath. The loveliest of scents were wafted across to me, the heart-piercing song of birds could be clearly heard and the whole vision seemed to promise the answer to my deepest longings as much as the sight of water to a desperately thirsty man. I ran towards this glorious world.[1]

The rest of the story of the dream tells of his being turned back from that heavenly vision. Years later, he could say: 'it remains as true and clear to me today as it was then'.

The Place

There are many places where the heart is strangely warmed – places of deep peace, of outstanding beauty, where some incident has occurred or where one can imagine an event of spiritual significance. For me, the temples of Kamakura, Japan, the garden tomb in Jerusalem, the jungle villages of Sri Lanka. All these leave memories which remain and are part of one's life. But what place has had the most profound effect upon my life? It has to be what was then (1935) a small village within pleasant walking distance from Oxford. It changed the direction of my life and always called me back when I had wandered from the path! It is called Eynsham. I was student-pastor there for two years. My earlier life had been devoted to science and I had already launched upon a scientific career. Experience in my church convinced me that I should study medicine and go to China as a medical missionary. I was accepted and had my plans to study medicine at Oxford with clinical training at St Thomas' Hospital, London. I had a scholarship and was ready to go. Then some doubts at the Baptist Missionary Society about whether I could stay the course led them to urge me to give my scholarship to a 'more suitable candidate' from an established Baptist family of missionaries. I went up to Oxford to study theology reluctantly! My college principal was the only one who seemed to understand. He was Dr H. Wheeler Robinson, a severe man, but very helpful to me. He allowed me to spend two of my years in the village of Eynsham as student-pastor. Of course, I neglected my studies and he understood. Gradually, the little Baptist community stole my heart. I found myself helping real people with real problems. There was a funeral, there was a harvest festival, there was a believers' baptism. Gradually I saw my first vision change – here was a place of healing and I was being used. I saw lives changed – I don't mean converted, important as that is – but sullen young people began to smile, families held together under great strain, love bound us together in a remarkable way. I knew then that my life was intended for the home ministry – not China, not medical work, but what the Germans call 'Seelsorge' and we call 'cure of souls'.

In 1938 I found a church just like Eynsham and they wanted me. After a while, the war broadened my pastoral work. Each church after that led to the reaching out that I knew I wanted. In St Albans, the German POWs descended upon us and they became part of our 'Seelsorge'. I had had many jobs since then – Senior Control Officer in occupied Germany, the BBC, the United Bible Societies and the World Association for Christian Broadcasting. But always that experience of a wounded student finding himself in Eynsham never left me. Each position I held became for me a pastoral one and whenever I could, I settled into a local church. Once I left the world stage, I settled in two successive churches, the ministries of which have covered the last 30 years of my life and I have felt the warming effect of that community of real people in Eynsham. Yes, Eynsham is the place that has had the most profound effect upon my life.

The Poem

In the rich garden of English poetry, there are hundreds of verses which blaze for a while and inspire the current experience. They grow dim but continue gently enlightening the soul. But for me, there is one that has come back again and again to burn afresh and light up my life. It is Shelley's *Mourn not for Adonais*. It is his poem on the death of John Keats at an early age. I first saw its beauty at Oxford when my closest friend, Ronald Bryant, read it to me with his voice bearing traces of his Welsh ancestry. He died young and when he died I read the poem with a new understanding. Later, in the midst of war, with young casualties reported every day, it came back to me. I was the minister of a church in St Albans for a time and we had evacuated to us two schools – Parliament Hill School for Girls and the Northern Polytechnic (all boys). They joined our youth club and I wondered how we could relate these two very different groups. The Northern Poly boys were pretty rough. One evening when we had had news of considerable casualties in London, I brought them together and read *Adonais* to them. It was a risk but it worked. They listened with rapt attention. The beauty of the words was not lost on them nor the need for many of them to understand the unity of life before and after death.

The first four lines of the poem are:

> Peace, peace! He is not dead, he doth not sleep –
> He has awakened from the dream of life –
> 'Tis we, who lost in stormy vision, keep
> With phantoms an unprofitable strife.

That stanza contrasts the passing of a spirit with the messy business of continuing to live – 'We decay'. And there follow such lines as 'He has outsoared the shadow of our night' and 'He lives, he wakes –'tis Death is dead, not he.' And then in a perfect description of the relationship of earthly life to eternity, using the image of the rainbow or Newton's spectrum:

> Life, like a dome of many-coloured glass,
> Stains the white radiance of Eternity.

Within that life beyond death lies all the colour of this earthly life, now completely unified. Since those days, I have conducted many funerals and this poem has often been in my mind and often quoted.

Now, as I come to the end of my life, it breathes life into the dull formulae of Christian creeds. Finally, let me quote a truncated stanza before the last:

> That Light whose smile kindles the Universe
> Burns bright or dim, as each are mirrors of
> The fire for which all thirst; now beams on me,
> Consuming the last clouds of cold mortality.

My Philosophy of Life

The foundation for this was laid in home and church. It has been much shaken over the years but never completely destroyed. When my mind wanders, the old mantra echoes in my head, 'Lord, Thy Word abideth and my footsteps guideth.' I have never completely abandoned the belief in a power which is directing and caring. None of the explanations of life without some faith in the beyond seems to make much sense to me. But I do not believe in a God who rescues me from the consequences of my own folly. I am not a fundamentalist but I still find the Bible a valuable guide to faith and action. I have no desire to be like any of the characters in the Bible but I find powerful ethical attitudes in the life of Jesus and would like my philosophy of life to accord with the Sermon on the Mount. I think the most powerful influence upon what philosophy I have is an insatiable love of life. That means that I love people and, if it is not beyond my power to awaken love in them, I want to do everything I can to help them. If I find someone I cannot love, I try to discover what is good in them. It is my conviction that there is something good in everyone. My evangelical faith, tattered and torn as it is, compels me to look at the worst and say, 'for that person, as for me, Christ died'. I don't think my philosophy allows for much discipline. My mother's half-truth comes too easily to me: 'If you really like it, it is bound to do you good.' Realising the dangers of such a philosophy, I impose certain disciplines and try to keep them but they must never impede the demands of love.

So how does this almost unstructured philosophy work out in practice? I try to apportion my life and my doings into three forms of passing the time: one third for creative work, one for routine activity, one for relaxation. It doesn't always work but it is a good pattern. If any one of those three takes over your life, it is destructive of a fully human life. A life of creative work – writing, preaching, broadcasting, translating etc. which fills every hour is destructive of the human spirit; a life made up entirely of routine practice of one's duty, even one's work, paralyses the initiative; a life of pleasure, 'unrest', 'what men miscall delight' (Shelley) saps the appetite.

I believe in God. I believe in the essential goodness of humankind and I believe in life with all its joys and colours. As is already clear from the previous gold ring, I also believe that life is a form of consciousness which passes, as at the end of a dream, into eternity. So far, this seems to have worked – I am enjoying being alive and I am not fearful of death.

MOTHER ROSEMARY

Mother Rosemary SLG (Rosemary Kemsley) was born in London in 1947. She studied at King Alfred's College, Winchester and then briefly taught theology at Queen's College, Harley Street. In 1971 she entered the Community of the Sisters of the Love of God, an Anglican contemplative community with its Mother House at Fairacres in Oxford which, since then, has been her home and spiritual family. She became Reverend Mother of the Community in 1996. She spent a sabbatical in 1991 at Amaravati Buddhist Monastery and for the last 12 years has benefited from the friendship and teaching of nuns and monks in the forest tradition of northern Thailand.

The Person

Granny Halahan

My grandmother was brought up in Norwich Cathedral Close at the end of the nineteenth century. Studio portrait photographs show her as a beautiful and fashionably dressed young woman, petite, with a small nose, high cheekbones, a clear brow and a determined chin. Her brothers called her Dollie. One day, the story goes, the fleet sailed into Yarmouth harbour and Dollie was invited to a ball on board the flagship. There she fell in love with a dashing young naval officer and he fell in love with her. They sailed to Malta together and were married in the Anglican cathedral.

When my grandfather took his bride home it was to a rectory in the remote south-west of Ireland. His father, bewhiskered and gaitered, used a donkey to ride over the hills to visit his flock. Buttermilk stood in big flat pans in the stone dairy; sanitation consisted of double privies where tall stinging nettles grew in the rough garden. On Sundays, the family went by pony trap to lunch with cousins at the big house. Then came the Troubles (the big house was burnt to an empty shell) and the Great War. After the war, Dollie had a difficult life as a naval officer's wife, moving often from port to port, often short of money and often, in effect, a single parent.

When my mother died (by then I had been a nun for 12 years) I was comforted by a little oval photograph of her as a baby in her mother's arms, taken in Ireland in 1907. Dollie in her lace choker and little pearl necklace, looked young and gravely innocent but it was as if she were saying to me now, out of deep wells of experience, 'It is all right. We can *carry* this unbearable thing, this death business, between us.' She died when I was a baby. She had been through the separation which death effects between a mother and her daughter; she had also lived through two world wars and huge changes in the way people live. She could tell me how birth and death are related, how it requires successive generations to bear them, and how the succession of generations requires both.

Later, I found two letters from Granny Halahan which my mother had kept. One was to my father, giving him permission to marry 'my dear girl' in 1943. The other was written to my mother when I was a very premature baby struggling for life in an oxygen tent. She wrote about prayer and about me:

> I think that if our faith leads us to pray to God, it must mean that we believe. He will hear us, and answer our prayers, and give us whatever He knows is best for us. But because we do not always get what we ask for, does not mean that God has not heard our prayers to Him. So we pray, trusting and believing in His merciful goodness, and knowing that with Him 'Nothing is impossible . . .' So many of us prayed and are praying daily to Jesus to spare your darling baby's life, and believed He would and could; so is not your little baby a direct answer to all those prayers, and our great faith.

So her prayer and faith may be more than a profound influence upon me. I may owe them my life. And to that ball in Yarmouth harbour I owe the particular bit of history that I am rooted into. It must stand for innumerable other 'chance' meetings and love stories, and their formative influence, in a family tree, upon the baby who survived.

The Book

The Book of Common Prayer

Even before I could read, the *Book of Common Prayer* gave me a language, which I am still learning, and connected me with a community. Sunday by Sunday, even if I was playing with my mother's gloves and thumping the hassocks, 'church' was going on all around me. This included the people buried in the churchyard and named on the stone memorials, as well as Jo Tucker, who led the Amens, Cecil Hough who read the lessons, and 'dear Mrs Shenstone', who sat in the pew behind us. The Prayer Book was a sort of portable church. At school we learned a good deal of the Prayer Book by heart. Before Matins on Sunday morning we learned the collect for the week, and every term we learned a psalm, as well as chapters from the Old and New Testaments. Learning the catechism was the basis of Confirmation classes. Reading and praying the collect, epistle and gospel from the Prayer Book was the basis of preparation for Holy Communion – and a good grounding in allowing texts to 'speak' to each other. Church was a lifeline of continuity between the worlds of school and home and between outer and inner life.

Much of what we read or sang in church I did not understand but I can still feel the excitement of some early breakthroughs into meaning. The Te Deum was always a high point but one Christmas day I heard as for the first time, 'day by day we magnify thee and we worship thy name ever world without end'. I knew about magnifying because we had a magnifying glass in a silver holder on the hall table at home. With it you could make printed letters loom up like jaws to eat you, or tame them to walk in docile readable rows. The magnifying glass could also beam light around the room like a torch, and I had seen a fire made with it. This is what the Prayer Book said we do with God. We make God bigger and bigger every day, then he blazes up (it can be dangerous) so that we worship him more and more, 'world without end', because there is no limit to the bigness of God.

The Prayer Book kept me company through adolescence, through ups and downs of emotion. Phrases from the psalms and the Communion service enabled me to explore feelings of longing and times of desolation, depths and heights. And I learned how seeking the right words to say to God is a search for truth and a way of prayer. Later I found how 'given' words in liturgy can take me in to experience held in common, supplementing and enlarging what is personal without denigrating it. At the heart of this activity is the connection which I learned first by hearing and experiencing it in church, between awe and love, and 'God'. Knowledge which otherwise would hardly be bearable had a name and could be spoken.

The Place

The Essex Marshes

Long before I walked between the Crouch and the Blackwater, I became familiar with the compelling quality of the marshes through an 'icon'. It had seemed a strange picture to be given pride of place on our dining room wall, just a small woodcut mounted on a large expanse of white board in a narrow wooden frame. The picture itself was no more than a line drawn on a pale aquamarine ground, and the slight lumpiness in the line was said to be a gun-punt. So there it was, space, a minimum of human interference just to give scale and a huge sky.

Later, when I went there, sound was added to the picture: the tide seeping through the mud, the cry of seabirds and the thud of their wings, and a steady, just perceptible vibration which could be coming from within myself. And the smell and feel of the wind, sometimes blowing straight from Siberia, and the taste of salt on my lips. And the light, constantly changing and calling forth a kaleidoscope of colours, even on the greyest day. For me, this is a landscape for healing, for giving sympathetic form to a mood, however subtle and wordless. I know my father loved it. It is a place where I can walk and breathe, and bear the changes of weather and circumstance; there is room in its beauty for pain to turn into joy. Walking by the Blackwater I have been opened and stretched by the sky, rested by the land and remade by the sea.

When I first went there in the 1950s, St Cedd's seventh-century chapel of St Peter's-on-the-Wall at Bradwell-juxta-Mare was being used as an implement shed. Since then it has been restored; it is the home of the Othona Community and is increasingly a place of pilgrimage. Amazingly, I have been able to go there again occasionally since becoming a nun. The chapel, foursquare, bleached and scoured by the wind, reminds me that the praises of God have been sung here by monks who made 'the dear face of Christ' visible in a country at the edge of the world, and where it had not been seen before. The feel of being on the edge of the unknown remains. The elements – earth, air, water and the fiery sun – are manifest in unadorned clarity, and it is as if fragments of the pre-Christian and non-Christian world unite with the communion of saints, as Roman bricks and local flints combine in the chapel walls.

The Poem

On a dark night,
Kindled in love with yearnings – oh, happy chance! –
I went forth without being observed,
My house being now at rest.

In darkness and secure,
By the secret ladder, disguised – oh happy chance! –
In darkness and concealment,
My house being now at rest.

In the happy night,
In secret, when none saw me,
Nor I beheld aught,
Without light or guide, save that which burned in my heart.

This light guided me
More surely than the light of noonday,
To the place where he (well I knew who!) was awaiting me –
A place where none appeared.

St John of the Cross

It still astonishes me that I am a nun, that I am here, that this community of Sisters exists and that I belong to it. Which is not to say that I always feel that I am in the right place or comfortable to be here. Certainly something, or someone, powerful brought me here and, astonishingly, I was able to make that step but quite soon afterwards I found myself in the midst of doubt, without a sense of God's presence and bewildered. I wondered if I had been mistaken, whether my hopes had been no more than wishful thinking. It was then that reading *On a Dark Night* I found in it the tale of my own experience. I had 'gone forth' (this is the Buddhist expression for taking on the renunciant life of a nun), led by a 'burning in my heart' and now, at the longed for place of meeting, there was no one and nothing.

This poem has helped me to go on trusting the light or guide that burns in my heart, even against the evidence and when to do so seems impossible. What is described is a metaphor for the discovery of a liberating secret, a relationship with God, the beloved, which is always moving on, though it is characterised by rest and stillness. Within this relationship, lyrically described in the rest of the poem, it is possible to acknowledge that there is something within me that cannot be denied and, at the same time, I am saved from taking myself and my limited perceptions too seriously. It is a way of escape from idolatry and stuckness.

St John uses the poem as the starting point for two volumes of detailed and penetrating commentary on the spiritual life in which faith opens the disciple to ever-deeper purification, untangling of complexes and more direct and simple dependence on God. Through the exercise of faith we may learn that darkness is not something to be feared. Sometimes it is a protective shield, and a necessary condition of God's activity. Sometimes darkness is itself a mode of God's self-revelation, adapted to our capacity to receive love, and stimulating us to love more. The poem challenges me to 'go forth' again and again, not necessarily dramatically, by an inward movement of relinquishment and hope.

My Philosophy of Life

Lord Jesus Christ, Son of the Living God, have mercy on me a sinner

I find that I am closest to truth when I receive everything as gift. 'What have you that you did not receive? If then you received it, why do you boast as if it were not a gift?' (1 Cor. 4:7). Empty-handed, I can receive life freshly moment by moment.

Part of the given, for me, is belonging to the Church and this is a gift that I want to enter into more and more. I want to make use of the opportunity that life-long familiarity with the Scriptures has given me, and to live in such a way that when I meet Christ face to face he will recognise me as a sheep of his flock. I have come to understand that though my knowledge of God is small, the more significant thing is that I am known by him. And with God knowledge and love are one.

Faced with the unfairness of my own good fortune in a world full of suffering and need, I turn to the cross and passion of Christ. Human capacity for pain is mercifully limited for there comes a point when we lose consciousness or die – but Christ? It was when watching a television programme about the dropping of the atom bomb on Hiroshima that I began to imagine how it might be for God with no pain threshold, no limit to his capacity for suffering, 'no limit to the bigness of God'. Christ prayed in Gethsemane in agony as he struggled to accept the given cup of human suffering and death, and Jesus *is* prayer, our union with God. At the very least that means that we are no longer alone anywhere. And if I am willing to go with Christ and experience, as he wills and as I am able, what he did by descending into hell and rising from there to fullness of life, can I perhaps contribute to what he has accomplished? That is a hope worth living for.

In retreat with Buddhist monks and nuns and sharing experience with them, I have learned to become more truthful about suffering and its extent throughout the conditioned world. Practically, if I resist the habit of pushing away my own small suffering I can learn from it how much suffering is born of greed, hatred and delusion. Seeking to follow the way of Christ and to live by the Christian monastic vows of poverty, chastity and obedience is a constant challenge to apply this insight. It helps me to recognise in myself a microcosm of the conflicts which afflict the world and to keep bringing the underlying disorder (my knowledge of it and my ignorance of it) to God. 'Lord Jesus Christ, Son of the Living God, have mercy on me a sinner' is uttered in solidarity with all, and in the power of the Holy Spirit it is also a celebration and a song of thanksgiving.

MARGARET SILF

Margaret Silf is an ecumenical lay Christian, committed to working across and beyond the denominational divisions. She is a native of Yorkshire but now lives in Stoke-on-Trent. A graduate of London and Keele universities, Margaret is married with one daughter and worked until recently as a technical author in the computer industry but is now engaged in writing and retreat-giving. She is the author of a number of books on Christian spirituality and is especially concerned to help free spirituality from its sometimes daunting theological language and imagery, and to 'earth' Christian faith in everyday living.

The Person
When a butterfly flaps its wings, the result may be an earthquake on the other side of the world. Such is the interrelatedness of all life. The proverbial butterfly created a flap when a cannon-ball shattered the knee of Inigo Lopez, the Spanish defender of the fortress of Pamplona. The earthquake hit me nearly 500 years later and I certainly wasn't the only one to feel the rumble!

The defeat at Pamplona was the beginning of a radical conversion for Inigo, later St Ignatius Loyola. He began to explore, and later articulate, a process of spirituality that has been life-changing for millions of spiritual pilgrims since that time, bringing the Gospel to life in a vivid new way and encouraging them to discover for themselves who God is for them and how they intend to act upon such discoveries. Ignatian spirituality has given me permission to doubt and to question, as well as to take the risk of trusting and loving, both God and God's world. So I acknowledge Inigo as the person who has had the most profound effect on my spiritual life.

Ancient wisdom, however, needs modern practitioners. Inigo's wisdom has been mediated to me very specially by two of his 'sons' – members of today's Society of Jesus, the order he founded. So I celebrate them too, with a depth of gratitude I find it impossible fully to express. They are Gerard Hughes sj and Brian McClorry sj.

Brought up in an agnostic household I was, however, sent to the local Methodist Sunday school, a decision for which I am now very grateful with hindsight. So when during my twenties I hit a personal crisis and urgently needed to rediscover the God of my childhood, I instinctively headed for the university chaplaincy. There, one bleak January Sunday morning, I walked straight into the hands of a Jesuit priest. It would be no exaggeration to say that I also fell into the hands of the living God. Today it's hard to believe how close I came to fleeing from both of them!

That Jesuit, Brian, has become a most cherished mentor and friend who has accompanied me through a whole landscape of uncharted spiritual territory where I would never have dared to venture alone. Already in that first encounter, he gave me a gift beyond price. He listened! He took my spiritual flounderings seriously. He gave me sacred space, with no agenda except that of welcoming love. I couldn't believe it. It turned my life around.

Gerry was to cross my path when he came to speak at Keele, preceded by his classic book *God of Surprises*. Several years later, Gerry accompanied me in making the sustained prayer journey of Ignatius' *Spiritual Exercises*. I count him among my dearest friends – a 'mover and shaker', a relentless provoker in the cause of justice and peace, and a man of great gentleness, humility and integrity.

Brian and Gerry taught me, above all, the importance of living true to oneself, of being authentic. If I have learned this lesson at all, I have learned it from their example.

The Book

I agonised over this one! Our home is lined with books. An impossible task to say which has most profoundly affected me. After drawing up my shortlist I surprised myself in the end by alighting upon a title that didn't initially appear there at all – a very unassuming little volume that I keep picking up and going back to and recommending to others. I'm not sure I would want to read it every day forever on a desert island but I do find so much in it that resonates with my own spirituality. Its title? *Jonathan Livingstone Seagull* by Richard Bach.

What does this story have that brought it to the top of my mind in the face of many, apparently much worthier, contenders? It tells the story of a little gull who intuits at an early age that there is a whole lot more to life than just surviving. He begins to test himself against his own limits – flying higher and higher. While most of the flock are content just to fly as far as the food supply and back,

Jonathan realises that flight is something worth doing for its own sake. Most of the gulls fly in order to eat. He eats in order to fly and fly and fly.

Jonathan is about the 'more' in life. Ignatian spirituality emphasises this 'magis' – the sense that there is always more beyond the horizon, that life as we see it is only a glimpse of something infinitely fuller – but that the quest for this transformative 'more' demands real and costly personal commitment. Jonathan is such an Ignatian gull!

Bach's parable spells out very graphically the cost of this commitment. Jonathan is stretched to – and beyond – his physical and psychical limits until he breaks through into new dimensions of consciousness. But there is also a social and political price to pay. The 'flock' – whoever they happen to be – will not easily tolerate the individual who flies free and challenges their own passive behaviour. The other gulls persecute and eventually exile him. Now an outcast, he discovers for himself that the quest for transformation can be a very lonely flight.

Perhaps, though, what speaks to me most in this story is the fact that Jonathan, having successfully and dramatically broken through to a transformed way of being and an eternal flight path, readily consents to return to the flock whose lives he has now transcended to teach those who are ready to be taught how they too can evolve beyond their earthly limitations. The outcast returns to lead the way for all.

Jonathan is, of course, a Christ-figure. He reminds me that the Christic vision can never be simply about personal fulfilment, nor some kind of individual passport to an imagined happy-ever-after. Nirvana, so Buddhist wisdom suggests, will not be achieved until the last blade of grass is redeemed. The prophet who flies on the edge of the flock does so for the sake of all.

The Place

I grew up in a suburb of the industrial town of Sheffield in the north of England. My parents rented a small semi-detached house in the district of Woodseats. We had a little garden that was my father's pride and joy. At the end of the garden was a fence separating us from a small footpath that led into a wooded area – Strelley Woods. The best thing about this fence was that it had a gap in it – not big enough to warrant a proper repair job but, happily, just big enough for a small girl to creep through. The gap in the fence was my gateway to heaven.

Once loose in the woods, I was in another kingdom. I made it my own. I was an only child and there were no other children of my age living nearby so from the start I was always a bit of a loner. Soon I knew every tree in those woods. I knew which of them could be climbed and which made good dens. I knew when the bracken would start to spring up and when it would be almost as tall as I was myself. The natural world was my nest and my playground. It was completely obvious to me then that God not only existed but that God lived in Strelley Woods. I couldn't understand what all the Sunday school fuss was about. You only needed to go to the woods and it was all there! And it is still the bedrock of my faith that God is in everything and everything is in God.

What did the woods teach me? Well it was certainly there, more than anywhere else that I discovered the gift of imagination. The trees and flowers, the birds and occasional animals were my play-mates and I made up the scripts as I went along. Sometimes the woods were a vast prairie to be explored or an ocean of new horizons to be sailed. Sometimes my favourite tree branch was a wild stallion upon whose back I rode the world, sometimes it was a resting place where I discovered another gift of the woods – the gift of reflection.

I guess I learned to pray there. I learned how it feels to be in awe of the moods and seasons of creation, of the wonder of growth, dying and new life. The high season of these liturgies always arrived in April, when the woods were carpeted with bluebells. At first I would gather these lovely flowers and put them in a jam jar to adorn my den or to take home for my parents. Then I would watch, grief-stricken, as they wilted by noon. The bluebells taught me never to try to put God in a container. It doesn't work. You kill the mystery as soon as you put it in a box, whatever holy name you inscribe upon the box.

But, thank God, Mystery – the real thing – is indestructible. Maybe that was the greatest gift I discovered in Strelley Woods.

The Poem
My choice of poem has to be R. S. Thomas' *The Bright Field*.

I have seen the sun break through
To illuminate a small field
For a while, and gone my way
And forgotten it. But that was the pearl
Of great price, the one field that had
The treasure in it. I realise now
That I must give all that I have
To possess it. Life is not hurrying

On to a receding future, nor hankering after
An imagined past. It is the turning
Aside like Moses to the miracle
Of the lit bush, to a brightness
That seemed as transitory as your youth
Once, but is the eternity that awaits you.

I know this field! I rather think we all know such a field if we delve deeply enough into the caverns of memory. It's a field that becomes radiant with transfiguration light every once in a while. Suddenly, for no apparent reason, we feel fully alive and we know that we have temporarily entered an invisible reality far greater – and more benevolent! – than our own little ego-world.

The field itself isn't a special place. It's just the ordinariness of the everyday trudge. It's the *light* that seems to make the difference. It illuminates all that has been and it makes a difference to everything that follows after.

I can look back over a few epiphany moments like this in my life and they have become touchstones for me in my spiritual journeying. One such moment was when I was just a small child. One winter evening I found myself transfixed by the immense expanse of a clear starry sky above me. I stood, rooted to the spot (I can still remember the place – still see the red telephone kiosk to my left and the old sweetshop to my right – still hear the buzz of traffic on the nearby main road) and simply gazed for I don't know how long. I remember feeling a sense of being so completely alone in this vast universe and yet also so completely at home – a sense of belonging, of being related to it, part of it – that has never left me but only grown stronger through the years. It was a moment that revealed to me for the first time 'the pearl of great price', long before I had any way of rationalising it.

There were other moments like this – not many, but enough to convince me absolutely of the reality of this invisible Otherness that envelops and penetrates the created world with what I can only call a loving presence. There was a moment out of time much later in my life, following on a period of turbulence and distress, when I awoke one November morning simply to feel myself bathed in this same warm awareness of belonging and of being unconditionally loved. I can't explain these experiences but research carried out by the Alistair Hardy Institute at Oxford into the nature of spiritual experience strongly suggests that they are widespread. The sadness is that most people never speak of their encounters with the Other, not quite daring to trust their own experience.

These moments in the bright field convince me of two things. They remind me that the real thing is always the Now, even though I spend most of my energy regretting or hankering for the past, or trying to anticipate the future. And they convince me of the reality of that Otherness I call God. No creeds and doctrines can ever capture this experience. When we allow the bright field to speak its truth to our hearts, we enter a presence that no one can ever negate or diminish. We *know* what we know. Such experiential knowledge, if we dare to trust it, is fuel for the spiritual journey.

My Philosophy of Life

Sometimes a phrase lodges in the mind and flatly refuses to leave. Such a phrase took over a permanent corner of my mind when I first read E. M. Forster's novel *Howards End* way back when, while I was still at school. The phrase in question was 'Only connect!' I have since realised that when simple phrases or incidents take hold of the hem of our conscious attention and refuse to let go, there is a reason. Something in the unconscious depths is shouting for a hearing. The moment has some treasure to reveal. It was around the same time, my sixth form years at grammar school, that I stumbled on another significant phrase that was to have a profound effect on my thinking in the years to come. This was the poet Keats' expression 'negative capability', meaning the willingness 'not to know', to live in mystery without feeling compelled to define, dissect and devour it.

The significance of these two depth charges is still revealing itself. Probably what disturbs me most in traditional religion is that it tends not to encourage these two intuitions to be taken seriously. Indeed, it can actually sever connections rather than nurturing them. Thus the 'sacred' and the 'profane' get put in different boxes and kept rigidly apart. 'Godstuff' can't mingle with the stuff of everyday living. And negative capability is not high on the agenda of churches who deal in unquestionable securities. 'Not to know' amounts to agnosticism – not a description most Christians would want to claim for themselves.

Spirituality on the other hand (especially Celtic and other native spiritualities and traditions such as the Ignatian and Franciscan) is all about connecting. It encourages the seeker to look for the strands of the divine in every aspect of ordinary living and to let that God-shimmer inform and transform all we do and all we are. It recognises the mystery that draws us always beyond the horizon of anything we can either understand or imagine. And even as I write this, I deplore the dualistic thinking within myself that sets 'religion' over against 'spirituality', because I know that whatever life is about, it will turn out to be both/and rather than either/or.

The shortest sermon I ever heard, and the most powerful, was simply this quotation from Empedocles who lived five centuries before Christ and came to a sticky end by falling into an active volcano: 'God is a circle whose centre is everywhere and whose circumference is nowhere'. This is an image that makes sense to me. It allows me to connect to the God at the core of my being, knowing that this same God is at the core of every other creature, connecting us all in the great web of life. It allows me to live with ultimate mystery, that has no circumference because it is without limits and I don't need to know the where, how and when of it. It allows me to live and grow in this wholly interconnected flux of mystery whom I call God.

ELIZABETH TEMPLETON

Elizabeth Templeton is a lay theologian who formerly lectured in philosophical theology at Edinburgh University. She now works freelance, lecturing,
writing, preaching and occasionally broadcasting. Her main current involve-
ments are with ecumenical developments in Scotland, interfaith dialogue and
adult education. In all these areas, her main concern is to re-empower
people to grapple openly and intelligently with questions of belief in our
complex, pluralist, postmodern culture.

The Person

The person who, more than any other, changed my sense of reality
is John Zizioulas, now Metropolitan of Pergamon, a global theologian and ambassador for the Ecumenical Patriarch in Istanbul.

When I first met him, he was a lay theologian newly arrived as a
colleague at New College, Edinburgh. He had been appointed to
teach patristics by a professor who *knew* how the truth ran from
Athanasius, to Calvin, to Barth; and all of us feared the worst from
this unknown Greek! So it was arresting to hear an incidental
comment, soon after his arrival, that the best twentieth-century
theologians the West had produced were the Existentialist atheists
like Camus and Sartre.

A new world began to unfold for me. At one level, it was the
world of classic Eastern Orthodoxy, especially of the Cappadocian
Fathers and Maximus the Confessor. But at another level it was the
most riveting and poignant and human and truthful exploration of
existence I had ever come across. When I had studied the Fathers as
an undergraduate, they were at best algebraic and at worst,
gobbledygook. But here, John could take any access point: the
impossibility of getting non-fluoride toothpaste in Boots or a
toddler's rage at not being in two places at once, and could move
into articulating the pathos and fragility and glory of our human co-
existence in a vulnerable cosmos. What had been 'mere doctrines'
jumped into embodiment; the nature of humanity, the precarious
preciousness of matter, the world's vocation to freedom and
communion, the person of Christ, the nature of the Church.

My last uneasy vestiges of the Calvinist constrainer of nature, the ringmaster of cause-and-effect, disappeared, an exposed travesty of the non-coercive inviter and lover of creation. Tidy, rulebound ethics dissolved into the haunting anomie of God's solidarity with creation, resourced by the communion of Father, Son, Spirit. The distances between present reality and eschatological longing stopped feeling like a nostalgic projection, and became an energising insistence on anger and pity at the world's entrapment in the forces of death.

I very rarely see John now and his writings are dauntingly tough. *Being as Communion*[1] is still in print and various articles can be sussed out in rather recherché ecumenical periodicals.

There are still many areas where I can't follow the arguments to what John sees as a seamless existential conclusion (for example, on the necessity of bishops for the identity of the church). But I trust him further than I understand him. There is not a day when I do not find my existence clarified or challenged by his reading of the faith, the tension between absence and presence in all meeting, between human capacity and incapacity, the ambiguity of space and time as mediators and frustrators of communion. Summaries must sound withered and abstract as many theologies are. John, more than any other person I know, makes theology a faithful, open encounter with whatever earthed and concrete situation he meets. The excitement and stretching and toughness of that unfinished engagement with God is still my most creative discipline.

The Book

So many books to choose from, precious and revisited! Kierkegaard, Berdyaev, my beloved Scottish poets, Dostoevsky, George Steiner's subtle explorations of transcendence. How do I settle on one? But if I must, it has to be Martin Buber's *I and Thou*, seminal for so much of my understanding of art, my sense of real relationship, my sensitive guardian angel in the dialogue between faiths.

This second gold ring connects in a way with my first! I had read Buber twelve years before I met John but an anecdote from the latter's childhood perfectly catches the issue about 'I-Thou' and 'I-It' relationships. John had a favourite toy cockerel and one day found it irreparably dismembered by his big brother. Charged with this murderous dismantling, the older child said: 'I wanted to know how it worked.'

I and Thou distinguishes between relationships which are basically about investigation, classification, objectification, mastery, and those which are about mutuality, the response to otherness as mystery or gift, being willingly 'out of one's depth'.

It was an English lecturer, Jack Rillie at Glasgow University, who introduced us to *I and Thou*. He was suggesting that the artist's relationship to the world, articulated in whatever specific work of art, was the manifestation of a unique and irreplaceable 'I-Thou-ness', a transfiguring exchange. There were, of course, elements of teachable craft, reproducible skills. But at the heart of the act of artistic creation was this wholehearted giving and receiving of attention and newness, communicated in a particular form.

What light this two-fold distinction has shed on my experience since! It is endlessly suggestive in the world of personal and political relationships. It helps to interpret abuse and exploitation. It challenges all forms of reductionism in the human sciences. It communicates the luminosity of any world in which another is truly loved. It insists on the preciousness of difference. The 'I' and the 'Thou' do not absorb each other or melt into some cosmic blob. But neither are they detached or separate. The dynamic of identity, to do with reciprocity, with what Levinas (significantly another Jewish philosopher) calls 'Alterité', is about particularity delighted in, not dissolved.

It's not that I'm forever reading *I and Thou*, but whenever I do, I'm startled by its power and freshness. New contexts and encounters shed fresh light on the book and vice versa. (For me, most recently, the experience of non-trivial interfaith dialogue has been a kind of sparring-partner with the book!) Rereading it is not about revisiting a formula. It's more like an empowering form of renewable energy which recharges my existence when it is at risk of becoming inattentive or complacent.

The Place

Gigha is a small Hebridean island, a couple of miles offshore from the mainland of Kintyre. Sheltered from the worst Atlantic storms by the bulk of Islay and Jura, it is often passed over by the rainclouds on their way to precipitation by the higher mainland hills.

It nestles like a small paradise. One car ferry shuttles to and fro several times a day. There is a spine of single-track road with a few

lateral tracks to crofts and hidden beaches of white sand. The
hedgerows are tangles of gorse and broom and honeysuckle and
rosehips and darting birds. Miniature hillocks of bracken and rough
grass give contour. Tractors chug on a handful of working farms.
There is one good, welcoming hotel, one post office/general store,
one primary school, one church and graveyard in use and another
older graveyard with an Ogham stone, one village hall, one Old
Boathouse Tearoom near the pier. Nothing is obtrusive or clamour-
ing. With its sweet air and translucent sea, the island has its own
magic. It's also special for me as the place where, in December 1970,
I knew I was in love with the man I was to marry. It's where we
would like to be buried.

The people of Gigha, in the wake of those in Eigg and Moidart,
have just bought back their island from the last of the feudal
landowners who owned the big house and the Gulf Stream-
nourished azaleas of Achamore Gardens. The spirit of pride and
commitment to this self-determination is palpable.

They have to find a lot of money to repay the bank loan but they
are in good heart, determined that the island's life must be sustained
in non-ruinous ways, compatible with the spirit of the place. (The
cluster of consumer outlets meeting the Iona ferry tourists is a
sinister warning!)

'God's island' is the likeliest translation of the name. It feels like
that. The islanders, however, are not sentimental. Depleted fishing,
the recent closure of the small creamery, the several farms unworked
and unstocked, the absence of work for young adults – all present a
microcosm of the problems of local rural economies in the face of
global capital.

But almost every time I visit Gigha, I think I taste what the first
and last day of creation is about – a place which feeds the senses
with beauty, on a scale where intimacy is possible between people
and environment, where anything which happens to anyone
impinges on the whole community, a place with time for being as
well as doing.

It is not, of course, paradise. Physical hardships and human distress
stalk small islands as well as big cities. But Gigha is uncluttered
enough for truthfulness about the joys and pains of life and death,
power and powerlessness. A good space, where nature hints at its
own transfiguration.

The Poem

So much of my nourishment comes from poetry that choosing *one* poem is like saying which breath of your body you would most like to celebrate. Whole heaps of poets tumble round my existence – Norman MacCaig and George Mackay Brown, Zbigniew Herbert, e.e.cummings, Blake, Langland, T. S. Eliot.

But if I must name one, it's a poem I have lived with since 1969, when Iain Crichton Smith published *From Bourgeois Land* (Gollancz). Like so many poets of his generation, Crichton Smith was a Gael (from Presbyterian Lewis) wrestling with the ambivalence of his love and hate of Scotland's religious and secular culture. The oppressive finger of God is never far away but Crichton Smith's poetry is life-affirming, touching the world with attention and tenderness and pity.

From Bourgeois Land recreates the smell of guilt, the distrust of colour and gaiety, the tidy conformity of church, school, suburbia, masking the glory and fragility of existence, the underlying violence in nature and the human heart. Yet in all the measured rage against the hypocritical repressions of the culture, there is no cynicism. Over and over again, beneath the façade of propriety, we are taken into disclosure of precious vulnerabilities, of potential flowerings of passion, rage, music and conviviality.

The final poem in *From Bourgeois Land* is untitled, but it is a kind of 'envoi' or bidding prayer to Scotland's children (a generation of whom Crichton Smith had nurtured as a headmaster of genius). It challenges them to defy the legacy of Knox in their spartan classrooms crammed with the virtues of silence, obedience, order and tidiness.

I return to it again and again. The final two lines, from the pen of a man deeply scunnered by religion as he met it is, for me, the most concise, vernacular Christology I know.

> Children, follow the dwarfs and the giants and the wolves
> into the Wood of Unknowing, into the leaves
>
> where the terrible granny perches and sings to herself
> past the tumultuous seasons high on her shelf.
>
> Do not go with the Man with the Smiling Face
> nor yet with the Lady with the Flowery Dress

Avoid the Crystal, run where the waters go
and follow them past the Icebergs and the Snow.

Avoid the man with the Book, the Speech Machine
and the Rinsoed Boy who is forever clean.

Keep clear of the Scholar and the domestic Dog
and, rather than Sunny Smoothness, choose the Fog.

Follow your love, the butterfly where it spins
over the wall, the hedge, the road, the fence,

And love the Disordered Man who sings like a river,
whose form is Love, whose country is Forever.

My Philosophy of Life

At the age of 20 I was writing confident philosophical credos about the nature of conscience, the right and the good, moral objectivity and respect for persons! As I approach 60 I have difficulty identifying anything as systematic as a 'philosophy of life'! I am distrustful of those who think they have reality taped, and wary of ideology, religious or secular. Thinking hard about big questions is exhilarating and trying to verbalise the thoughts without banality or pretentiousness is a challenge. But I can't get much beyond 'assorted findings to date' which may hang together experientially but hardly amount to 'a philosophy' of anything! So, here goes:

- One needs to be hospitable to all one's experience and, above all, not to run away from dark corners. There is nothing which cannot be faced.
- People are ragged and wonderful beings. The human condition is full of joy, terror and pain. To live truthfully involves entering all that contradiction without tidying it up.
- What is unmanageable about our existence is likely to be more important than what we can manage.
- Growing in grace involves embodying the recognition that I am not able to dissociate myself from anything or anyone else in creation.
- Nature, including human nature, needs transfiguration beyond the

moral if the 'integrity of creation' is to be realised. Space, time and causality need transformation as well as hearts and wills.

- The condition of the heart, the mind, the will, are mutually inter-connected. Desires, beliefs, intentions, hopes, commitments cannot be isolated from one another without 'disease'. The imagination of love is more important than reason.

- Language is the most wonderful, dangerous gift. To avoid speech falling into ideology, it requires the constant scrutiny of con-versation, dialogue, decoding, reformulation, silence. At its best, it is a vehicle of shared, articulate life.

- (Formulated by Ian Fraser, former Warden of Scottish Churches House, Dunblane): 'Life is for risking, not hoarding.'

- Many kinds of spiritual introspection and self-improvement agendas are pretty narcissistic. Genuine spirituality is ecstatic, going outwards towards the other, self-forgetful.

- Candour and tenderness are not incompatible. Furtiveness about disagreement is, in the long run, poisonous, worse than anger.

- The transparency of small children is a paradigm of personhood.

- Fullness of life has to do with the convergence between freedom and communion.

MARK TULLY

Mark Tully KBE was born in 1935 and worked for the BBC from 1965 to 1994 as the BBC Representative in Delhi, Chief Commentator for South Asia for the World Service and as the BBC South Asia Correspondent. Now a freelance broadcaster he has presented *Something Understood* on Radio Four since 1995. In 1985 he received the Bafta Dimbleby Award and the Order of the British Empire; in 1997 he was awarded an honorary doctorate of the University of Strathclyde and in 2002 he was awarded the KBE. He is an honorary fellow of Trinity Hall, Cambridge.

The Person

There have been so many people who have influenced my life that it is very difficult to choose one person. I was particularly fortunate in the priests of the Anglican church I knew when I was young and I owe a great debt to all of them. There was the chaplain of my school John Miller, then Bob Runcie my tutor at Cambridge and after him Alan Webster and Tom Baker at Lincoln Theological College. All these were prominent churchmen but in a strange way the person who influenced me most deeply was the vicar of the small country church I attended during school holidays, Philip Francis of All Saints Marthall, Knutsford, Cheshire. No one could call Philip a prominent churchman and that is what impressed me so much.

Philip was a small man, thin too, with a few wispy hairs. He was a bachelor but being of a low church persuasion not a committed celibate. He lead the services in a high-pitched tone far removed from the wonderful rich voices of so many cathedral clergy. Sociability did not come naturally to him but my father became enormously fond of this shy reclusive man and he used to bring him home for dinner after evensong on Sunday. In that way we all came to know Philip, to learn of his hidden sense of humour and it would not be going too far to say that we came to love him as a member of the family.

At that time I was at a highly competitive public school. It was an early indoctrination into the cult of success and success defined very narrowly. Philip represented the opposite of all that. He was the vicar of a small church with no ambition to go higher in his profession or to be given a larger and more prestigious parish. He was not particularly successful if attendance at church was to be the measure of that but it never worried him. What attracted me was his perseverance in the faith without looking for any reward and his loving care of those who did open themselves to him. I had an uncle who suffered brain damage at birth. He would visit us at least twice a year and was so devoted to Philip Francis that he never missed a service. Philip always invited Uncle John to tea on his own and that was the highlight of his stay with our family. There was what was known as an 'epileptic colony' in the parish, Philip ministered faithfully to the patients. He usually held services in the colony but on rare Sundays they came to All Saints and I could see the affection they had for Philip.

So what was his impact on me? Philip's example led me to believe that the peace of God can never be found by those who lack humility, by those who aspire for greatness. Philip believed in fulfilling his vocation as well as he could and leaving rewards and judgement to God. I could not claim to have lived up to his example but in my ego-bruising profession whenever my ego has been bruised I have thought of Philip. Sometimes I have also thought of him in moments when my ego was in danger of inflation.

The Book

The book I return to time and time again is not the Bible, not the Gita in spite of all that Hinduism has taught me, not Shakespeare but the *Book of Common Prayer*. Every year I buy the Church Book and Desk Diary, not because I ever take services or am even as regular in my attendance at church as I should be but because it means that I get to read the collects every Sunday and every major saint's day. Of course I have my favourites. The long spell after Trinity has some of them which remind me that I am in debt, that as the collect for the seventh Sunday puts it so memorably God is the 'author and giver of all good things'. The ninth Sunday forces me to admit that I cannot do anything which is good without God, and the collect for the twelfth Sunday recalls God's generosity and my ingratitude with the reminder that God is 'always more ready to hear than we to pray'.

The collect that sticks in my mind most firmly is, not surprisingly one I have heard most often, the collect for Advent Sunday said every day in Advent. It stresses the humility of Jesus and I find humility, when achieved, a most comforting virtue, a virtue which enables me to be the person I am, not to strive to be someone different or even, dare I say it, someone better. Because there should be a tension in life between tradition and change, between the past and the future because I believe we are in danger of being, as I heard one Roman Catholic preacher warn, 'drunk on change', I love the collect for the Sunday next before Advent, traditionally known as Stir Up Sunday. The collect calls on God to 'stir up the wills of his faithful people so that they may plenteously bring forth the fruit of good works', and tradition calls us to stir up the Christmas pudding with plenty of fruit on that day too.

But the *Book of Common Prayer* means more to me than the collects. The liturgy became part of my life when I was young and I have somehow found myself going back and back to it in times of disarray, distress and disobedience to God. My love of the liturgy is not rational, I don't want to examine the wonderful words too closely. They are beautiful and mysterious, as God is. Recently I attended a Eucharist in an Anglo-Catholic church where the priest celebrated with the utmost reverence and the mystery of the sacrifice was heightened by a magnificent choir. As I received communion I was struck by the thought 'I don't care what this means, I just know it means a great deal to me.' Loose theology or lack of theology like that may be deplorable but it sums up the power of the liturgy for me and that is why the *Book of Common Prayer* has been so important in my life.

The Place

I am not very good at sightseeing, have a limited tolerance for monuments and museums, and moved though I am by many artists I find no picture painted inspires me with the sense of awe that nature does, so my favourite place has to be somewhere of great natural beauty. But then I am not much of an athlete and don't like trekking long distances, wrestling with waves, or shooting down ski slopes, so the place has to be somewhere I can be peaceful. That is why Chail, a small town in the western Himalayas, is a place I go back and back to.

At 2226 metres above sea level Chail is high enough to provide awe-inspiring views of the snow-capped peaks and the foothills of the Himalayas, ridge after ridge rolling down to the great Gangetic plain. No photograph or film can capture the many-coloured monsoon sunsets – they have to be seen to be believed. The scent of the pine forests is purer than any perfume. To become part of the mountains I need time to change, to relearn the art of peaceful living – a day outing is not enough. Chail does provide peace too. It's not on a main road so the small town isn't choked with traffic fumes and my ears are not deafened by the cacophony of Delhi's traffic. My eyes, too, are not offended as they are in better-known Himalayan towns like Shimla and Darjeeling which have been over-run by hotels, shops and restaurants – ugly concrete buildings bearing no relationship to the architecture which tradition taught was best suited to the mountain terrain and climate, or to the pretty little-England style the British brought to their hill stations. Chail only has a modest bazaar and a hotel which is not unlike an English country house – it was the summer palace of the Sikh Maharaja of Patiala. The hotel is comfortable without being ostentatious and the tariff is tolerable, it doesn't trouble my peace of mind.

But Chail, for me, is more than a destination for a relaxing holiday. Both mighty mountains and a stormy sea fill me with a sense of my unimportance. They dwarf any human achievements. They are primeval, far older than we are. We can deface the mountains with our constructions and indeed destruction, but somehow their majesty remains. We can cross the sea in ships, mine it for oil and befoul its waters with the debris we create to meet our needs, yet those turbulent windswept waves will always be magnificent: stretching to the horizon, they demand reverence and respect. But although mountains and the sea inspire awe and humility they do not belittle us. When I stand beside a small Hindu shrine on a mountaintop above the forests of Chail I do indeed feel very small but I become aware that I am not without significance. I belong, I am part of nature and have my place too. Wordsworth remembered,

> There was a time when meadow, grove and stream,
> The earth and every common sight,
> To me did seem,
> Apparelled in celestial light.

He ended that first verse of his poem *Intimations of Immortality from*

Recollections of Early Childhood, with the line 'The things which I have seen I now can see no more'. I do see them sometimes on that mountaintop near Chail.

The Poem

For more than 30 years I have watched the historic city of Delhi expand from a manageable population of three million to perhaps thirteen. I have seen the change from a city of bicycles to a city choked by the fumes of the internal combustion engine. Where I live is now surrounded by slums, filthy and inhuman. I have reported futile efforts to clean the sacred River Ganges and met peasant farmers displaced to make way for power stations which are not going to benefit them because they can't pay for electricity, and dams which will flood their fields. The Mughul Emperor Jahangir described a royal progress through Central India as like 'travelling from garden to garden'. Were he to make the same journey today he would barely see a flower or a tree.

The defilement of Delhi, the desecration of the Ganges, the denuding of the land, all this can't be blamed on India. India is just following the West's example, pursuing economic growth without considering the cost, turning a blind eye to the damage of consumerism and competition and treating the world as though it was ours to do what we like with. It's just that the results of this misunderstanding of the true nature of our world are more devastating in a country like India in which poverty is still prevalent. Distressed by what I see all around me I turn to Gerard Manley Hopkins' poem *God's Grandeur* for a true understanding of our world, an understanding which does not lead to despair.

The Jesuit priest's poem starts 'The world is charged with the grandeur of God'. It is God who charges the world with the energy that upholds it – an energy without which all the energy we generate and use would be of no avail, the world would fall apart. The grandeur is there for everyone to see. Hopkins says 'It will flame out, like the shining from shook foil.' After asking 'Why do men then now not reck his rod?' he goes on to describe, with something akin to disgust, what we have done with God's world: 'All is seared with trade; bleared, smeared with toil / And wears man's smudge and shares man's smell.' In saying immediately after that 'the soil is bare now, nor can foot feel, being shod' Hopkins is surely explaining why we have smeared, seared and smudged the world, why we have not recked God's rod – our feet are no longer on the ground, we have lost touch with nature.

But as a Christian the poet cannot despair, he must have faith in God's mercy and his power so he writes, 'And for all this, nature is never spent: there lives the dearest freshness deep down things.' For all our greed we will never exhaust nature, 'Because the Holy Ghost over the bent world broods with warm breast and ah! bright wings.' So I need not despair of India or the West and I can hope that one day we will, like the poet, hear the beat of those wings.

My Philosophy of Life

To say that I have a philosophy of life would suggest that I have found all the answers to living. I haven't. I believe that life is one long search and that we will never reach certainty. What we can strive for is to find a path through life, but that means reading the signs along the way, being open-minded. I see certainties as danger-ous, leading to disputes rather than dialogue, to distortion rather than truth and, all too often, if honestly questioned, to disillusion-ment. Living in India with its ancient multi-faith tradition I lost the certainty that Jesus is the only way and that no man comes to the Father but by him. I came to realise that there must be many ways to God. But the loss of that certainty strengthened my conviction that there is a God. After all if many different ways, discovered in dif-ferent parts of the world, in different cultures at different times, all lead to similar experiences of God doesn't that strengthen the case for a divine creator with whom we can communicate? What's more, many roads fit in with human nature too. The Dalai Lama when asked why there are four different schools of Tibetan Buddhism, replied, 'because there are at least four different types of people'. It seems to me that Christians should rejoice that Jesus has manifested himself in diverse ways to diverse people, rather than try to bind themselves together in some uncomfortable institutional unity.

So how does one live with uncertainty? A Hindu friend of mine has suggested that balance is the key. Learning from years of study-ing the Mahabharata, he described the balance the Hindu epic teaches in these words:

to value the material over the spiritual or the spiritual over the material, the transient over the eternal or the eternal over the transient, the body over the mind, or the mind over the body, the individual over society or society over the individual, the self over the other or the other over the self, is to create conflict both within oneself and with the rest of the world.

So a balance also has to be sought between certainty and uncertainty. For me that has come to mean accepting that Anglicanism is a certain way because it has led so many people to God but not a way which denies the validity of the experiences of those who have taken different routes. Mahatma Gandhi once said, 'In spite of my being a staunch Hindu I find room in my faith for Christian, and Islamic, and Zoroastrian teaching.'

Gandhi believed he should live as a Hindu because that was the religion of his birth, it was his fate to be a Hindu. In finding room for other faiths he was balancing fate with the free will to choose. To me that is one of the most important balancing acts we are called upon to perform, to accept fate without becoming fatalists and to accept free will without coming to believe we are entirely in charge of our own destiny. Acknowledging the need for balance between fate and free will, accepting that I am like a tight-rope walker always in danger of losing my balance, I have come to the conclusion that life has to be a continuous search for balance rather than the stationary stability of certainty which is stagnation.

ROBERT TWYCROSS

Robert Twycross graduated from Oxford University Medical School in 1965 and was appointed Research Fellow in Therapeutics at St Christopher's Hospice, London in 1971. He returned to Oxford in 1976 as Medical Director of Sir Michael Sobell House, a palliative care unit at the Churchill Hospital. In 1988 he was appointed Macmillan Clinical Reader in Palliative Medicine, Oxford University, a post he held until September 2001. Since then he has continued as Emeritus Clinical Reader. He is also Academic Director of the Oxford International Centre for Palliative Care and Head of the World Health Organisation Collaborating Centre for Palliative Care. He has written over 250 articles, chapters and editorials and is author of several books.

The Person

Dame Cicely Saunders, born in 1918, and generally regarded as the founder of the 'Hospice Movement' of the late twentieth century. After reading philosophy and economics at St Anne's College, Oxford, she trained as a nurse at St Thomas' Hospital in London. Later, she became a lady almoner (medical social worker), also at St Thomas' Hospital.

As a result of her work there, she came to recognise that, if terminally ill patients were to receive adequate care, the negative attitudes of most doctors in relation to such patients needed to be changed. In stark contrast to the chilling phrase 'There's nothing more that I can do for you', she became convinced that there was always something that could be done to ease a patient's pain and other discomforts, and sense of social isolation. As she later said:

> You matter because you are you.
> You matter to the last moment of your life.
> And we will do all we can
> not only to help you die peacefully,
> but to live until you die.

A senior physician told her that only if she herself became a doctor would she be able to change medical attitudes. So, in due course, she applied for a place at medical school, again at St Thomas'. She qualified in 1957 at the age of 39. A year later, she began to work with the Irish Sisters of Charity at St Joseph's Hospice, Hackney and started to make plans to build the home she had first dreamed about years before. And so, in July 1967, St Christopher's Hospice in Sydenham, South London, welcomed its first patients.

I first met Cicely Saunders in 1963 when, as a medical student at Oxford University, I attended an International Congress of the Student Christian Movement. I attended a series of seminars there on healing and health – also attended by Cicely as a medically qualified facilitator. What she said about 'hospice care' with its emphasis on the psychological, social and spiritual needs of the patient, as well as the physical, made an indelible impression on me. Physical comfort remained important, of course, and she spoke of the need for the regular prophylactic use of painkillers and other symptom-relief drugs. More specifically, she described the correct way to use morphine by mouth and how to counter its adverse effects. What she said appealed greatly to me and, in 1964, I invited her to lecture in Oxford. We subsequently corresponded inter-mittently and in 1971, after several years in general medicine, I was appointed Research Fellow in Therapeutics at St Christopher's Hospice.

About the same time, the National Society for Cancer Relief (as Macmillan Cancer Relief was then called) began to work in partnership with the National Health Service to build units in NHS hospitals dedicated to what later became known as 'palliative care'. And so in 1976 I was appointed Consultant Physician to Sir Michael Sobell House, a new NHS in-patient palliative care unit at the Churchill Hospital, Oxford. Over succeeding years, I helped to develop the service into one incorporating specialist community nursing, out-patient and ward consultations, day care and bereave-ment support. At the same time, I wrote and taught extensively about palliative care. In 1988, I moved sideways into a university post while continuing to work as a physician at Sobell House ... all because of Cicely Saunders.

The Book
Apart, of course, from the Bible and the works of Shakespeare. Perhaps surprisingly, my choice is a book which was my idea and in whose production I played the major role, namely, *Mud and*

Stars: the impact of hospice experience on the Church's ministry of healing.[1]

The working party met over a three-year period between 1989 and 1991. About 20 people were involved, comprising clergy from several Christian denominations and health care professionals. Most of the latter were palliative care doctors and nurses, and the clergy were either hospital chaplains or otherwise associated with the church's ministry of healing. For me, the working party was a powerful stimulus to wider reading than my job normally allowed. It enabled many feelings and thoughts to emerge into the light of day and to exposure to the searching comments of other working party members. As a result, my hospice experience and my beliefs became integrated into a more healthy coherent pattern. Many of the cumulative psycho-spiritual stresses from my work ameliorated, though not without considerable psychosomatic disturbance.

It was necessary to ensure that the working party report clearly reflected the string of paradoxes which emerged in our discussions. As a title, *Mud and Stars* seemed a good fit: 'Two men looked through prison bars; one saw mud and the other stars.'

Mud symbolised the concomitants of a physically messy death, i.e. one complicated by incontinence, vomit and/or blood, and *stars* reflected the experience of many patients and families, namely that the illness had drawn them together and even that 'the last year of my life has in many ways been the best'.

As someone said, 'You can't die cured but you can die healed.' The discovery that the Hebrew word *shalom* (peace) implies a sense of well-being and completeness, irreducibly both individual and corporate, and stemming from a positive state of 'right-relatedness' to, and dependence on, God was the entry point for me into a rich reservoir of stimulating ideas.

The Place

I worked at Sir Michael Sobell House for over 25 years. You cannot work in the valley of the shadow of death for most of your professional life and accompany several thousand people in their Gethsemane without it having a profound effect on you. For me, it meant the end of Christian 'triumphalism' and led to a deep sense of humility. I now prefer expressions like 'the Gospel of Anger' and 'the Gospel of Weakness and Failure'. I know for certain that the certainties of youth are an illusion and that faith and doubt are inseparable. I continue to wonder why the Church Fathers omitted a vital phrase from the creeds, namely, 'We believe life is unfair'.

In a hospice, one is forced to face the facts of life as they are, not as we might wish them to be. All around us, everyday, there are endless examples of arbitrary suffering. One poignant example was that of a 68-year-old man dying of lung cancer. He had four children, three girls and one boy. All the girls suffered from an inherited disease which led to liver failure. One died as a teenager, the second survived to marry but died in her mid-twenties, the third had a liver transplant and is still alive. The son was not affected. Then, two or three months after the father was diagnosed as having terminal cancer, the son was killed in an accident. And so I am forced to share the despairing cry of those who suffer:

Why God? Why? Why, when our need
is desperate, when all other help is vain,
do you turn away from us?

Why? Why, when the darkness is deepest
and our midnight is starless,
do you hide yourself from us?

Why, in times of grief and distress,
when there is no light in the window,
do we find a door slammed in our face,
and a sound of bolting and
double bolting on the inside?

Why forsake us when we need you most?
Why are you present when the skies are clear,
our help in days of prosperity,
but so absent in our time of trouble?

We know that faith does not exempt us from sorrow
or shield us from evil – we know that; we know too,
that the earth is wet with the blood of the innocent –
but why this? Why now? Why?

Know this, God, know this: if faith were dependent
on feelings, if our trust in you were no more than

> a matter of the mind, we would have done with you,
> done with you now, done with you for ever.[2]

To accompany someone who is dying means staying with them in their experience of forsakenness and despair. I must not try to hurry them through the complex journey of adjustment and acceptance. Fortunately, in this task I am sustained by a deeply held belief that there *is* more to the story:

> God of Christ,
> God who raised him from the dead,
> God with whom life can begin again,
> come to us now, hold us, help us, heal us,
> for you and you alone are our salvation.[3]

Even so, being 'honest to God' and being angry with him is a necessity for me. Without this avenue of release, I could not have continued as a hospice doctor. I need to be angry. I thank God that, in his infinite capacity to love and to give, he is able to absorb all my anger and still more. In this respect, I think of God as the Celestial Garbage Can.

The Poem

At different times different poems have provided inspiration. Writing this after three weeks in South Africa where, with my wife, I witnessed the impact of the AIDS pandemic engulfing sub-Saharan Africa, I would nominate a poem written by Margaret Hichens after a friend had disclosed her HIV-positive status:

> *Friends*

> We are told we must have a positive outlook on life.
> Take time to admire the Jacarandas, smell the earth after the
>   first rain,
> and listen to a baby's gurgling laugh.

> But suddenly it seems life is really positive: HIV Positive
> And everything changes.
> It is hard to be positive in one's outlook and attitude,
> when being positive in this HIV way,
> means the beginning of the end.

That long lonely slow painful journey into despair, anger and
    bitterness has begun.
The Jacarandas don't matter, rain is just rain,
and why bring babies into this world
if we deny them a proper family with both a mother and a
    father?

But wait. Someone does care.
Someone understands how I feel and doesn't mind if I want to
    scream,
Or smash a plate or swear

I am not alone.
There are others prepared to reach out and take my hand,
to touch me and to hold me.
We can laugh together and weep together, our tears mingling
    as our laughter did.

Is this what being positive about being HIV Positive is all
    about?[4]

This poem emphasises the depths of despair and isolation, of alien-
ation and forsakenness, experienced by the sufferer but also stresses
the hope and emotional strength received through friendship. This
message is relevant to all who suffer and, at some stage, this means
all of us.

My Philosophy of Life

> 'The philosophers have only interpreted the world; the point is to
> change it.' (Karl Marx)

My father was an Anglican priest. Family life revolved around the
Christian liturgical year and Sunday worship. You could say that I
was born religious. I cannot remember a time when I did not 'say
my prayers' and I remember my elder sister introducing me to daily
Bible reading when I was eight. I have never doubted the existence
of God and have always accepted Jesus as 'the Word of God'.

    Inevitably, therefore, my philosophy of life has been a Christian
one, with love of God, love of neighbour and love of self as its

essence. All I have attempted and achieved stem from this foundational belief. However, I am human and the right balance between the three objects of my love has often, perhaps mostly, been distorted to my seeming immediate advantage. On the other hand, my understanding of Jesus' message ('The time has arrived; the kingdom of God is upon you. Repent, and believe the gospel') has changed dramatically since I moved into palliative care in 1971.

Caring for the dying is not easy. A former colleague described it as 'extremely harrowing but very rewarding'. It is difficult but, para-doxically, there is generally a positive spin-off. This helped me to appreciate that truth itself is paradoxical, e.g. cross and resurrection, suffering and joy, trouble and peace, doubt and certainty. I now see that belief and doubt are not opposites but that doubt is the middle ground between belief and rejection. As someone said, 'Doubt is faith in evolution' and 'Where there is doubt, there is hope.'

Another paradox: the end is always a new beginning. Indeed, the gift of the Holy Spirit means that I have an enhanced potential for change and personal growth. This is both liberating and threatening because I find that I am constantly being called into the unknown by He who is all-knowing. Cardinal Newman once said, 'To grow is to change, and to be perfect is to have changed often.'

For me as a hospice doctor, a God who suffers is an essential belief. What is God like? *God is like Jesus*. Christianity is not about an empty cross and an empty tomb. It is about – simultaneously – a crucified Christ and a risen Lord. The two must be held side by side if we are to be true to the insights of the New Testament, in which Jesus is described as 'The Lamb slain since the foundation of the world' (Rev.13:8).

Others have repeated this theme. Pascal said 'Jesus will be in agony until the end of the world', Lev Gillet asserted 'The cross is eternal. There was a cross in the heart of God before there was one planted outside Jerusalem', and Studdart Kennedy claimed 'My only real God is the suffering Father revealed in the sorrow of Christ'. And St Paul said 'The whole created universe in all its parts groans as if in the pangs of childbirth' (Rom. 8:22). Thus:

> To seek God, who is the fount of life and love, is no easy option; indeed, the path to God will, contrary to cosy

traditional Christian reassurance, open us up to more, not fewer, conflicts. In turn our greater openness to the trials and failures of human life and love will make us in the end more open and more vulnerable, more capable of being hurt as people. Yet our very vulnerability through openness, our ability to accept and welcome tensions in ourselves as ultimately un-resolved and unresolvable, are our passport to wholeness and happiness and, in the end, the keys to the Kingdom of God.

Anon.

BERNARD WEATHERILL

Bernard Weatherill was born in 1920, he was educated at Malvern College and served in the Second World War. He was employed in the family business of Bernard Weatherill Ltd, Tailors of Savile Row, London from 1946–70 and became President of the Company in 1992. From 1964–92 he served as MP for Croydon NE, from 1967 to 1979 serving in the Whips Office and as Deputy Chief Whip to Edward Heath and Margaret Thatcher. From 1979 to 1983 he was chairman of the Ways and Means Committee and Deputy Speaker. He was chosen as Speaker from 1983 to 1987 and again, unanimously, from 1987 to 1992, and from 1992 to date has sat in the House of Lords as Convenor of Independent Cross Bench Peers. He is a member of the Fellowship of St John.

The Person

Politicians are sometimes lampooned as 'Devils elected by Angels' but the truth is very different – we are a cross-section of the nation and parliament contains many more saints than sinners! I have been a member of the Society of St John the Evangelist's Fellowship of St John for well nigh 50 years – long before I entered parliament and I will always be grateful to the good Fathers in St Edward's House who have been my spiritual guides and have massively influenced my attitude to life.

Looking back however, the person who has had the most profound effect on my life was – it may sound trite – my mother and to a lesser extent, my father.

My father was born in 1883 – one of eleven children. He contracted poliomyelitis at an early age and as a result had little formal education – he was trained as a tailor as a means of survival. In 1912 he was prominent in a strike to improve sweatshop conditions in tailoring workshops and was thereafter unemployable. He was forced to set up on his own account and I am proud that the family business which bears his name (and mine!) is now a prominent one in Savile Row. I learnt from his example courage and determination and resolution – and from my mother 'a stiff upper lip'.

My mother was born in 1886 and by contrast was highly educated and cultured. She was sent to Leipzig University in 1904 and subsequently trained as a nurse in Bart's Hospital. In the First World War she was one of very few nurses to serve with Allenby's army in Mesopotamia. She was formidable, strict but kind, and had strong suffragette tendencies!

However, I was a problem to them. I steadfastly refused to eat meat! This was considered so unacceptable that it was decided that I needed discipline and at the age of seven was sent off to a boarding school where I sat next to the headmaster at every meal and remained at table until I had forced down the meat! Eventually a wise and eminent doctor pronounced that this was unnecessary cruelty and when I went to Malvern College I had vegetarian food.

Alas this was even worse! Failure to be part of the pack led to a miserable existence and I left in 1938 with a singular distinction – 'The Senior Inferior' – deemed and doomed to fail! But looking back this turned out to be a worthwhile bonus and a blessing. It has left me with a genuine sympathy for the underdogs in life, but also a determination to prove to my parents and to the world that masters were wrong in their assessment.

So the profound effect of those persons may be summed up in A. P. Herbert's poem:

> A certain school in days gone by
> Contained two pupils, x and y.
> Young x was what you'd call a swot
> Whilst y most definitely was not.
> Young x spent all his time of leisure
> In reading classics just for pleasure,
> Whilst y frequented football grounds
> And helped the milkman on his rounds.
> All this was fifty years ago;
> Success may seem a trifle slow,
> But it will come if we await
> With patience the decrees of fate.
> Young x is head of that same school
> Whilst y, whom masters thought a fool
> Is owner of a chain of stores
> And Chairman of the Governors.[1]

When I eventually joined the School's Council the business had 16 branches!

The Book

I joined the army in 1939, in the Oxford and Buckinghamshire Light Infantry, and quite by chance found in Blackwell's a copy of Emerson's *Essays*. It was the only book that remained with me throughout my army service – five years in the Indian Army.

There have been many masters of wisdom but Emerson has the gift of an interpreter – his essays on self-reliance and compensation and manners and character and, above all, love have helped to shape my life.

To talk about love in our society is not considered 'manly' but it is difficult to find a more appropriate word to express the bond of genuine respect and affection we had for our Indian troops and they for us. Just one example – shortly after we landed in Burma I woke one morning during the monsoon to find that I was dry – I looked again and saw four pairs of feet – four young jawans (soldiers) were holding a groundsheet over my slit trench. It was an experience I will never forget.

Of course I did have the advantage of being a non-meat-eater, a bond we shared, but more than that was the bond of genuine trust and affection, and the knowledge that if one led from the front they would follow!

The Place

Without a doubt – India. As soon as I stepped ashore in Bombay in 1940 I felt at home.

Today I am a firm believer in reincarnation and I am in no doubt that this was the reason. I quickly mastered Urdu and was fortunate enough to travel widely and to remote districts.

When I entered parliament as MP for Croydon NE I was unaware that for over 100 years Addiscombe Seminary had been the training college of the Honourable East India Company – it was the heart of my constituency.

In Northern India in 1942, I came across a tomb bearing the name of a young HEIC official which had become a shrine. I cannot recollect his name but I noted his memorial, still visible: 'He was trusted – absolutely.' This memory came to me out of the blue shortly after I was elected Speaker of the Commons in 1983 and I adopted it as my motto. I pray that I lived up to it.

The Poem

I was brought up in a Christian household but in recent years I have been influenced by Buddhist traditions – largely as a result of my friendship and admiration for the Dalai Lama. Christians are taught 'Whatsoever a man soweth, that shall he also reap'. I believe that each incarnation is a training ground for the next, until we reach Nirvana – union with God. In the words of John Masefield:

> I hold that when a person dies
> His soul returns again to earth
> Arrayed in some new flesh-disguise –
> Another mother gives him birth.
> With sturdier limbs and brighter brain
> The old soul takes the road again.[2]

My Philosophy of Life

My philosophy throughout forty years in parliament has been shaped by Mahatma Gandhi's 'Seven Social Sins':

> Politics without principles
> Wealth without work
> Pleasure without conscience
> Knowledge without character
> Commerce without morality
> Science without humanity
> Worship without sacrifice

These words, written in 'Young India' in 1925, are engraved on his funeral pyre in Rajghat, New Delhi.

When I was chosen as Speaker in 1983 I was persuaded by my chaplain – Trevor Beeson – to talk to the Parliamentary Christian Fellowship on 'The Christian in Politics'. Politicians should be wary about entering pulpits, bearing in mind the dictum of Ralph Waldo Emerson: 'The louder he talked of his honour the faster we counted the spoons'! However these words from an address I gave in St Margaret's, Westminster probably encapsulate a little more precisely my philosophy of life:

> If what Christians say about God is true, then everything in life matters to him. On that basis alone it can be maintained that

politics matter to God and that they should therefore matter to the people of God. As Max Warren has put it: 'God is a God of politics. Only if he is a God of politics and social life dare we at all worship him in church. For to worship in church a God who is not a God of politics and who is not as much concerned with what happens in the market place as what takes place in the sanctuary, is to worship an idol and not a living God.'

Christians must therefore get involved or else abandon all political influences to agnostics and atheists. To be in public life is to enjoy an opportunity to influence people on a great scale. In our lifetime the State has become the most comprehensive institution of society. This being so, the Christian cannot justifiably ignore politics any more than he can avoid politics as a citizen. In many parts of the world the State has become the most threatening incarnation of the Prince of Darkness. Great segments of mankind live constantly on the brink of disaster because political power is in the hands of godless politicians. Christians therefore have a duty to involve themselves in politics; to seek to ensure that political power is wielded with wisdom and compassion and, above all, to ensure that it is used to liberate and not to enslave. The modern politician has the power to influence so many of the evils that have cursed mankind for countless generations. No Christian is entitled to curse darkness when it is possible for him to carry such a torch.

In Lamb's biography of Alexander the Great, he recalls that in the course of one campaign Alexander and his Generals sat down to study their charts and found to their astonishment that they had marched completely off the map! To a large degree this is true of the technological age in which we now live. Our modern 'torches' shed precious little light on the enormous changes we are likely to see in our lifetime. But Christians do have a chart and one which has never failed them – the Holy Bible, and notably the Ten Commandments.

The cornerstone of good government has always been good people – not just at the top but in all levels of society.

'To make a Nation truly great, a handful of heroes capable of great deeds at supreme moments is not enough. Heroes are not always available and one can often do without them. But it is essential to have millions of reliable people. Honest citizens

who steadfastly place the public interest before their own.'
(Pasquale Villari, 1826–1918)

King Solomon, faced with similar problems to our own,
prayed not for power to overcome them but for the wisdom
to know the difference between right and wrong. *Nothing that
is morally wrong can ever be politically right.* If Christians subject
every political decision to that test, we shall have a country
which, in the beautiful words of the Communion Service, is
'Godly and quietly governed'.

ALEX WEDDERSPOON

Alex Wedderspoon was born and bred in Scotland, the son of a minister in the Church of Scotland. He was educated at Westminster School, Jesus College Oxford and Cuddesdon Theological College and was ordained in 1961. In the 1960s he lectured in religious education in the University of London and served as Education Adviser to the Church of England Board of Education. In 1970 he was appointed Canon Residentiary of Winchester Cathedral and Vice Dean in 1980 before becoming Dean of Guildford in 1987, a post he filled until retirement in 2001.

The Person

A good man, full of the Holy Spirit and of faith

My father was one of that ill-fated generation who came to maturity in the summer of 1914. In that year he graduated from the University of Glasgow intending to enter the ministry of the Church of Scotland. Instead, like many another, he found himself in the Army where he saw active service in the Middle East.

Surviving the war, he was eventually ordained to a grim mining parish in Lanarkshire during the years of the Depression. There he worked amidst poverty and destitution of a kind which is now unimaginable. In 1938 he moved to a suburban parish in Glasgow where, throughout the stressful years of the Second World War, he ministered single-handed to a large congregation at a time of constant uncertainty and sadness. As his eldest son was on active service as an RAF pilot, he had anxieties of his own but those he kept to himself. In 1945 he was persuaded to move to a church near London, where he died, burnt out, at 59.

He was a gracious, scholarly, courteous, kindly man with a fine sense of humour and twinkling eye. It never ceased to astonish me that he had been a soldier. He was a distinguished preacher and a forgiving and perceptive pastor. How he coped, single-handed, with the incessant demands of a large congregation, I shall never know. He had no secretary or any other kind of assistance. Like most Scots of his time, he took the view that life was hard and had to be lived with courage, endurance and good humour.

Whether or not he and my mother were happily married, I have no idea. Husbands and wives in the Scotland of that time did not keep questioning the quality of their sex lives and personal relationships. They stuck together to survive and for the sake of the family.

One of the great regrets of my life is that when I came of an age to appreciate him, he was already in terminal illness, which he endured without complaint. He was a man who in his life radiated the graciousness of a gracious God. I remember him with love and honour his memory.

The Book

Memory Hold the Door *by John Buchan*

John Buchan, Lord Tweedsmuir (1875-1940) was a man of astonishing talents and immense ability: barrister, colonial administrator, publisher, business executive, soldier, director of Reuters, Member of Parliament, Governor General of Canada. On top of this life of action and achievement, he was also a scholar, historian, prolific writer and highly successful novelist.

His autobiography was written from the heart and from memory – as the title suggests. When he wrote it he was in Canada; all his diaries and personal records were at home in England. In perfect English he tells of his love for the Scottish Borders and the landscapes of South Africa; his love for the University and the countryside of Oxford; his love for parents and family; his love for friends who fell in the First World War. He reflects on the events of his day and on the future of the church and civilisation he toiled to uphold and fought to defend.

Unlike many who write autobiographies, he relates no gossip and speaks no ill of any of his contemporaries. He makes light of his long struggle with failing health. He was a man beloved and respected in his time. Many books have been written about him and all speak of him with a kind of affectionate wonder.

I cannot lay claim to even a fraction of his brilliance but to a limited extent I followed in his path and know something of the life he lived and the places he cherished. I too went from Glasgow to Oxford, developed a respect for the British Army, worked for some time in London and came to know Canada. But there any kind of association ends. He was one of the twentieth century's finest men, a most rare personality, great in ability, faith, character and achievement. I read this book every year and never fail to be moved, strengthened and inspired.

The Place

Winchester Cathedral, Close and College

For 17 years I was privileged to serve as a Canon Residentiary, then as Vice Dean of Winchester Cathedral. Around the Cathedral there is a group of ancient buildings of exceptional beauty and historical importance: the Cathedral Close, Kingsgate Arch, Winchester College, Wolvesey, College Street, Kingsgate Street and the Wykeham Arms. Mercifully, the developers and the improvers have been kept away and the Dean and Chapter have not – yet – decided to sell the Close houses to stockbrokers and merchant bankers.

Walking around this part of Winchester on a summer evening, after the tourists have left, is to enter what seems like an enchanted world. But what matters is not so much the peace and beauty of the place as what that wondrous cluster of buildings represents.

The Cathedral and its continuing ministry affirms all that is best in the central traditions of the Church of England: dignity, order and beauty in worship; excellence in music; scholarship, reason and honesty in teaching; wisdom and compassion in pastoral care. The buildings of the College affirm every aspect of intellectual enquiry, study and sound learning, the disciplines and delights of music, drama and the arts.

Mahatma Gandhi was once asked what he thought of Western civilisation. He replied, 'I think it would be good idea.' But the Mahatma never visited Winchester. The cluster of buildings around the Cathedral represents everything that is not squalid about the world in which we live. It is a place of civilised and cultured living. Inevitably there are those who criticise it as being elitist and effete. But there is still the Wykeham Arms where the locals delight to gather in all their intelligent and cheerful naughtiness and in the warmth of their humanity.

The Poem

A Red, Red Rose

Archbishop Donald Coggan used to say that love matters because, ultimately, love is all there is. Robert Burns wrote about love from a wide and varied experience. C. S. Lewis, with godly intent, tried to departmentalise love into affection, friendship, eros and charity, but his scholarly analysis was not convincing. Love is a jewel with many facets but it is all one. This poem by Robert Burns expresses something of love's mystery and extraordinary power.

> O My Luve's like a red, red rose
>> that's newly sprung in June:
> O my Luve's like the melodie
>> that's sweetly play'd in tune.
>
> As fair art thou, my bonie lass,
>> So deep in luve am I
> And I will luve thee still, my dear,
>> Till a' the seas gang dry:
>
> Till a' the seas gang dry, my dear
>> And the rocks melt wi' the sun!
> I will luve thee still, my dear,
>> While the sands o' life shall run.
>
> And fare thee weel, my only Luve,
>> And fare thee weel a while!
> And I will come again, my Luve
>> Tho' it were ten-thousand mile.

My Philosophy of Life
My philosophy of life focuses around these affirmations, drawn from various sources:
- God is spirit and they that worship him must worship him in spirit and in truth.
- Jesus Christ, the same yesterday, today and forever.
- It is strange to be here, the mystery never leaves you.

- Our lives are filled with blessings and with awe.
- Look how wide the East is from the West; so far doth he set our sins from us.
- Praise the Lord, O my soul, and forget not all his benefits.
- The Kingdom of God is within you.
- Now abideth faith, hope and love and the greatest of these is love.
- All acts of love and pleasure are my rituals.
- In the garden of every life there is always the thorn.
- Be strong in trust, both in sorrow and in joy.
- God sees us with pity, not with blame.
- We are not human beings having a spiritual experience, but spiritual beings having a human experience.
- And all shall be well and all shall be well
  All manner of thing shall be well,
  For the Lord loveth us and ever shall.

Ringlets

RICHARD HARRIES

Richard Harries has been Bishop of Oxford since 1987. Before that he was Dean of King's College, London. He has been a parish priest and a lecturer in Christian doctrine and ethics. He is a Fellow of King's College, London, an Honorary Doctor of Divinity of the University of London, a Doctor of the University of Oxford Brookes University and a Fellow of the Royal Society of Literature. The Bishop has written 20 books including *Art and the Beauty of God* (Mowbrays, 1993), *God Outside the Box: Why Spiritual People Object to Christianity* (SPCK, 2002) and *After the Evil: Christianity and Judaism in the Shadow of the Holocaust* (OUP, 2003). He has contributed to a wide variety of national newspapers and journals. He is a regular broadcaster on radio and television and is well known for his contributions to *Thought for the Day*.

The Person

The person who has had the most profound effect on my life is my mother. I believe that in my early days, months and years I was warmly embraced, affirmed and cherished. Nothing later in life could compare with this influence which has given me a sense of my own identity and worth. My mother said she lost interest in children when they began to develop a mind of their own and certainly she was very different from myself! But nothing can be more precious than that early experience of bonding.

The Book

The book which has had the most effect on my life is Dostoevsky's *The Brothers Karamazov*. This wrestles, as no other book does, with the fundamental issue of evil and suffering and how, if at all, they can be reconciled with belief in a loving God. It set an agenda which is still with us. Dostoevsky is fair to all points of view, indeed I have seen a lecture entitled 'Will the real Mr Dostoevsky stand up?'

The Place

A place I value greatly at the moment is Burford Priory, where I go to spend quiet days. This is an Anglican religious community of both men and women. The worship is simple but beautiful, at once highly disciplined and sincere. The setting is miraculous, not least when the acres of snowdrops are out.

The Poem

The poem which has most inspired me is T. S. Eliot's *Four Quartets*. This faces the bleakness of so much life, the predominant theme of Eliot's earlier poetry. But it suggests that there is something beyond emptiness at 'The still point of the turning world'. Its haunting imagery and rhythms continue to reverberate in the mind. It is a poem that takes history and human experience generally seriously but it suggests that in and through them eternity can touch time.

My Philosophy of Life

As far my philosophy of life is concerned, I take seriously the fact that God has given the world a real independence. Indeed to be created at all is to have a life of one's own. Because he respects the freedom he has given the world as a whole and human choices in particular, he does not perform the miracles we so often long for. People continue to die too young and millions of people through-out the world suffer injustice. But God is working all the time to bring good out of evil and has given us the decisive sign of this in the crucifixion and resurrection of Jesus Christ. His purpose is not simply to increase pleasure and diminish pain, important though these are, but to help us grow in our capacity to love. Because this love comes in the end from God himself what is rooted in love cannot be destroyed. So life points beyond itself to its consummation in the communion of saints.

JULIA NEUBERGER

Rabbi Julia Neuberger is Chief Executive of the King's Fund – an independent health care charity which works to improve the health of Londoners by making change happen in health and social care. She was educated at Newnham College, Cambridge and Leo Baeck College, London. She became a rabbi in 1977 and served the South London Liberal Synagogue for twelve years before going to the King's Fund Institute as a Visiting Fellow to work on research ethics committees in the UK. She was Chairman of Camden and Islington Community Health Services NHS Trust from April 1993 until November 1997. She has been a member of the General Medical Council, the Medical Research Council, a Trustee of the Runnymede Trust and a member of the Board of Visitors of Memorial Church, Harvard University. She holds honorary doctorates from ten universities, is an honorary fellow of Mansfield College, Oxford. She is the author of several books on Judaism, women, health care ethics and on caring for dying people.

The Person

The person who probably had the greatest influence on me was my paternal grandmother, a woman who started her married life working in girls' clubs and nurseries in the East End of London as a middle-class volunteer but got her meaning in life out of being chairwoman of the Welfare Committee for the Refugee Committee for Jews from Nazi Germany from 1933 until the end of the war. She taught me idealism, devotion, bloody-mindedness, service and that one does not always have to be liked.

The Book

The book that probably had the greatest influence on me was Richard Titmuss' *The Gift Relationship* about blood donation and altruism. He was a wonderful man.

The Place

The place that probably has had the greatest influence on me is home – where I grew up in London NW3 – surrounded by love, books and pictures. I still think love and a devotion to scholarship in a place one can call 'home' is the best place from which to start.

The Poem

The poem that has been most influential for me is the section of Proverbs 31 from the Hebrew Bible (Old Testament) about the ideal woman. I have always wondered whether it is a true ideal or tongue-in-cheek by a secret feminist.

My Philosophy of Life

The philosophy of life that has driven me comes from the Hebrew Bible again and from the Mishnah (second century). It combines Isaiah's rage at the rich who ignore the poor, the instruction in Deuteronomy that one cannot hide oneself away from responsibility and the strong sense of urgency in the teaching of the Mishnah: 'The day is long, the work is hard, the workers are slowing and the master of the house (God) is pressing', with the requirement at least to make a start on the task even if you cannot finish it.

EPILOGUE

I have been asked during the course of this book's preparation – what of my own five gold rings? And while I cannot claim the eloquence of many of the contributors who have given so generously of their time and thought, nevertheless I offer the following:

The Person
Father Alan Cotgrove of the Cowley Fathers, Oxford, who, many moons ago, while I was spiritually ill at ease in the somewhat claustrophobic, shallow, negative, all-forbidding strictures of some aspects of fundamentalism, lifted me out of the doldrums and onto the sunny plains of a much broader, all-encompassing, deeper Christianity which transformed my life. He helped me to acknowledge that God being Love loves all that He has made and therefore life with all its richness and splendour, could be a far fuller, all-embracing, deeply meaningful experience than perhaps my teenage shallow fundamentalism had allowed. Each one of us has to find our own spiritual level, as it were – some are more comfortable with an evangelical, others a catholic tradition; some a liberal, others a conservative approach; others still need to withdraw as monks or nuns giving their lives to prayer and service, others to the deeper approaches of contemplative spirituality. I owe an enormous debt of gratitude to Alan.

The Book
Love is My Meaning – the brilliant anthology edited by Elizabeth Basset is a book crammed with truly inspirational spiritual gems that are fundamentally changeless in times of rapid change. I have turned to it again and again and it never fails to uplift.

The Place
St Cuthman's (formerly St Julian's) is a superb retreat house in

Coolham, West Sussex to which I have fled for rest and succour on many occasions. It is a house set in extensive grounds with its own lake, sublimely peaceful in the heart of Sussex. The vast panelled library probably contains the finest collection of books of any retreat house in this country and the simple chapel with its picture window overlooking the lake defies description. At this place I have come in prayer to make many life-changing decisions and for me it represents a very special place of rest and renewal.

The Poem
William Wordsworth's *Lines Composed a Few Miles Above Tintern Abbey* – the central section of which encapsulates so beautifully the mystic's intuitive certainty of God:

> ... And I have felt
> A presence that disturbs me with the joy
> Of elevated thoughts; a sense sublime
> Of something far more deeply interfused,
> Whose dwelling is the light of setting suns,
> And the round ocean and the living air,
> And the blue sky, and in the mind of man:
> A motion and a spirit, that impels
> All thinking things, all objects of all thought,
> And rolls through all things ... [1]

Hard indeed to find lines more sublime and powerful than these.

My Philosophy of Life
And so to my fifth gold ring – not so much a philosophy, more a credo, which is simply that:
- With John O'Donohue I believe we are spiritual beings on a human journey rather than human beings on a spiritual journey.
- I believe that here on earth through the joys and heartbreaks of each character-building event or experience, we are given the opportunity to become the kind of person God alone knows we have the potential to become.
- I believe that during this journey called Life, a journey towards God, we meet with very significant spiritual people who draw alongside us for a period, helping us to 'a closer walk with God'. My own life has been punctuated by meetings with such people

– some are with us only briefly, others for the duration.

• I believe that we should value solitude and silence – that essential life-giving succour to be found only when we draw apart:

> Many people today look for silence, solitude and peace. They dream of places where they can rest away from the daily hassles of living which tear them apart, exhaust them and leave them dissatisfied, wounded and bleeding and always alone. But they won't necessarily find peace and quiet waiting for them in other places. There is a place within us where quiet reigns – the centre, our heart of hearts. There we can find him who is the plenitude of silence. But who will guide us there? We must learn the way.[2]
>
> Michael Quoist

I will let Frederick von Hügel have the last word:

> Live all you can – as complete and full a life as you can find – do as much as you can for others. Read, work, enjoy – love and help as many souls – do all this. Yes – but remember: Be alone, be remote, be away from the world. Then you will be near God.[3]

AFTERWORD

When we come to the end ... believing that He ... will be able to take what we have done for Him, whether explicitly or implicitly and will gather it into His Kingdom, to be in that Kingdom as that particular enrichment of the Kingdom's glory which our particular life has to contribute.

For there is something which only you can bring into the Kingdom.

Eric Abbott (Dean of Westminster), *The Compassion of God and the Passion of Christ*

O God, in whom nothing can live but as it lives in love, grant us the spirit of love which does not want to be rewarded, honoured or esteemed, but only to become the blessing and happiness of everything that wants it; which is the very joy of life, and your own goodness and truth in our soul; who yourself are love, and by love our Redeemer, from eternity to eternity.

Amen.

The Devout Life: William Law's Understanding of Divine Love

NOTES

Marcus Braybrooke

1. Hans Jonas, 'The Concept of God after Auschwitz' from A. Friedlander (ed.), *Out of the Whirlwind* (Schocken Books, New York, 1976), pp.465–76.
2. This is the first verse of a poem quoted by A. C. Bouquet in *The Christian Faith and Non-Christian Religions* (Nisbet, 1958). I do not know the author.

Neil Broadbent

1. William Law, *The Spirit of Prayer & the Spirit of Love*, edited by Sydney Spencer (James Clarke, Cambridge, 1969).
2. William Law, *The Devout Life: William Law's Understanding of Divine Love*, edited and introduced by Israel and Broadbent (Continuum, 2001).
3. Alan Watts, *Behold the Spirit: A Study in the Necessity of Mystical Religion* (Vintage Books, 1972), pp. 74–5.
4. M. Israel with N. Broadbent, *Learning to Love* (Continuum, 2000).

David Clark

1. See *The Holocaust and the Christian World* edited by Carol Rittner, Stephen D. Smith and Irena Steinfeldt (Kuperad, 2000).
2. *The Marriage of East and West* (Fount/HarperCollins, 1982).
3. See *Mysticism* by Evelyn Underhill (Oneworld, 1999).
4. Demeanour, also demesne.

Denis Duncan

1. William Barclay, *Daily Study Bible* (St Andrew Press, Edinburgh).
2. Cameron Peddie, *The Forgotten Talent*. This book was last published by Arthur James but is now out of print.
3. The home will be built on the estate of the Duke of Hamilton in Dirleton, East Lothian. The Lin Berwick Trust is based at 4 Chaucer Road, Sunbury, Suffolk, CO10 1LN.

Joyce Huggett

1. The 10/40 window is a term used by missionaries to describe the area of the world with the largest population of non-Christians. The area extends from 10 degrees to 40 degrees north of the equator, stretching from North Africa to China.

2. Jim Borst whose book now bears the title *Coming to God* (Eagle, 1992).
3. This method of prayer has been described in detail in many books including my own *Open to God* (Eagle, 1997) and *The Smile of Love* (Hodder & Stoughton Religious, 1990).
4. Gerald Priestland's commendation of *God of Surprises* (Darton, Longman and Todd, 1985).

Robert Llewelyn

1. Robert Llewelyn, *Julian Then and Now: The Mercy and Forgiveness of God.* This can be obtained from The Julian Centre, St Julian's Alley, Rouen Road, Norwich, NR1 1QT.
2. The unceasing prayer of the heart is commonly pursued through the frequent repetition of some short prayer of which the best known is the 'Jesus Prayer', for which see *The Way of a Pilgrim* translated by R. M. French (Triangle/SPCK, 1930).
3. *Agape*, the characteristic New Testament Greek word for love, may be defined as an unconquerable goodwill towards another, likeable or unlikeable, friend or foe.
4. Compare with chapter 3 of the anonymous fourteenth-century classic *The Cloud of Unknowing*.

Edwin Robertson

1. J. B. Phillips, *Letters to Young Churches* (Fontana, 1971).

Margaret Silf

1. R. S. Thomas, 'The Bright Field' from *Collected Poems 1945–1990* (J. M. Dent, 1993).

Elizabeth Templeton

1. John Zizioulas, *Being as Communion* (Darton, Longman and Todd, London/St Vladimir's Seminary Press, Crestwood, 1997).
2. Iain Crichton Smith, extract from *From Bourgeois Land* in *Selected Poems* (Carcanet Press, 1985).

Robert Twycross

1. R. G. Twycross (ed.), *Mud and Stars: the impact of hospice experience on the Church's ministry of healing* (Sobell Publications, Oxford, 1991).
2. T. Falla, 'He is hidden' from *Be Our Freedom Lord* (Lutheran Publishing House, Adelaide, 1981), pp. 88-9.
3. Ibid.
4. M. Hichens, 'Friends' from *Living in an HIV + World: South African Stories of Pain and Hope*, edited by D. Gennrich and P. Sherriffs (uMngeni AIDS Centre, South Africa, 2002), p. 29.

Bernard Weatherill

1. A. P. Herbert, 'A Certain School in Days Gone By' from *The Book of Ballads, Collected Light Verse* (1948).
2. John Masefield, 'A Creed' from *Selected Poems* (Sinclair Stevenson, 1999).

Anna Jeffery (epilogue)

1. William Wordsworth, *'Daffodils' and Other Poems*, selected and introduced by Dominique Enright (Michael O'Mara Books, 2002).
2. Michael Quoist, *With Open Heart*, translated by Colette Copeland (Gill and Macmillan, 1983).
3. Frederick von Hügel, *Letters from Baron von Hügel to a Niece*, edited with an introduction by Gwendolen Greene (J. M. Dent, 1928).